Essays & Essais

DNM Architecture

Foreword, Essays and Acknowledgements by
David Marlatt, AIA
Preface by Xavier Soule
Principal Photography by
Jamie Leasure, Joseph Schell, Tyler Chartier, Andre Bernard, Antoine Trichereau, Open Homes Photography

OSCAR RIERA OJEDA
PUBLISHERS

CONTENTS

Foreword
David Marlatt, AIA

I am an architect, and I think of myself as a humanist. There are many definitions of humanist (it makes sense that there would be), but among the shortest I have found is "an approach to life based on reason and our common humanity, recognizing that moral values are properly founded on human nature and experience alone." As a self-defined humanist, I tend to accept people as they see themselves, assume they know more or less what is best for them, and do what little I can to help them along their way.

As a "humanist architect" (as opposed to a humorist-architect, which is just a hobby) my work is less concerned with adherence to a given style, advancing a school of architecture, or defending an idiom. It is mainly concerned with facilitating people as they navigate their environment and use buildings for whatever purposes they are suited. This is not the same as the "client knows best" or blindly following orders, far from it. If the client really knew best, they could be their own damn architect. Clients come to architects because they don't know what to do and often architects have to deliver bad news. Moreover, the people that we are facilitating in our work are not just clients and their families, but everyone who will interact with the building and everyone else potentially impacted by the building's very presence and carbon footprint. In this way, architects are analogous to doctors. A patient seeks out a doctor to diagnose some kind of ailment, and frequently hears some bad news at first. Then the doctor prescribes the treatment, not the patient.

Translating this approach to practice into design, I think of architectural styles as silos representing such movements as Modernism, Roman, Edwardian, Art Deco, International, Victorian, Mountain Rustic, Bungalow, etc... Many architects identify themselves by one silo resulting in a body of work that is consistent, easily recognizable and an ongoing refinement of that given style. Certain clients seek out these architects precisely for this reliability and happily subsume their own requirements to be part of a larger movement or collect a trophy.

But no matter what style or "silo" a work of architecture, or any art form, belongs to, it can also be classified as simply good or bad. Imagine that spanning across all of these vertical silos of architectural style are broad horizontal bands representing a spectrum of quality from bad to good. This is where most people live and circulate – often unknowingly and uncaringly – from one silo to another as it may suit their needs and desires. Styles are defined academically and can be evaluated objectively by comparing current works with historical precedents, writings, and occasional theory. Good or bad design, however, is judged empirically. A building works well for the people who use it or it doesn't, no matter the style badge it may be wearing.

If there is a consistent thread to our firm's work during almost 25 years of practice and hundreds of projects, it is that we have placed the practical needs of clients and their communities first. We conceive of the floorplan as a diagram for living and try to anticipate how the building will live over time. In another essay, I quote Mark Twain about his own house. *"to us, our house ... had a heart, and a soul, and eyes to see us with; ... it was of us, and we were in its confidence, and lived in its grace and in the peace of its benediction."* Put a less poetically, the house is an extension of its users. Through organization of spaces and myriad other design decisions, it anticipates and facilitates movement and delivers emotions that are needed – coziness, security, elation, energy, aspiration, and more. For homeowners, the house becomes a character in their own play.

In practice, we do "diagnose" the problems presented by a client's site, program, and budget, but architecture is more than just solving problems. It both addresses reality and expresses aspiration. We solve problems, but our work is foremost an attempt to honestly reflect and project our client's lifestyle and priorities rather than to fit them into a preconceived architectural style.

If almost all our completed work lands safely within the "contemporary" or "modern" zone, it is not a coincidence or an agenda. It turns out that people of the 21st century live have 21st century lifestyles, with their modern stuff and modern habits and modern tastes. They drive late model cars, almost always have two careers, work sometimes from home, stream movies and order out using Doordash. They are concerned about their impact on the environment, their children's futures and just saving money on utility bills. They are less concerned with societal hierarchy and more fluid in their relationships.

They are influenced by car and fashion marketing mantra that teaches "less is more" (ironically an expression originating in architecture). While it may be theoretically possible that an "honest reflection of our clients' lifestyle" based on these criteria, results in a Palladian villa or Victorian gingerbread house, those clients would be very strange time travelers indeed.

Our approach to design can be messy, highly iterative, and ambiguous – just like people! We joke that "design process" is an oxymoron. Rather than moving in a straight line, design is more like riding on the rim of a large wheel. In one dimension, it feels like moving backward and forward as the wheel rotates. As long as the rotation also moves in one direction, however, the project advances. We use analogies and metaphors a lot (analogies are like metaphors, a garden of ideas).

Style silos, diagnosis, personification, analogies, metaphors, rotating wheels… these are only terms for devices to smooth the winding road to great buildings. At the end of the day, they are just convenient tools without inherent value. Only built work counts as Architecture. Everything short of construction, whether drawings, renderings, or scale models, is a representation of what might be. We work to build, and our clients hire us to get that done for them. As a team, we make their dreams manifest. Often the buildings include ambiguities, some unresolved details, and some placeholders for potential change. There can be something like a symbiosis between spaces and the people who occupy them. We try to build those opportunities. After the project is complete and the architect and contractor have moved on, our greatest goal is that a client experiences their building over time and, for whatever reasons thinks "this is me."

Preface
Xavier Soule

I met David in Paris under the glass and steel vault of the Grand Palais, a unique icon of eclectic 19th century architecture. David was a young architect just arrived from Atlanta, and I was a slightly older architect from Paris who had graduated under this same mythical vault years earlier. At the time, we were not very effective in our Franco-American linguistic exchanges, but we both spoke architecture and plunged shamelessly into the fabulous CAD revolution of the 1980's that was just beginning.

A few decades later, we are now veterans of that revolution, but we still practice architecture, especially David. He speaks through his realistic utopias, the things he has built.

Among themselves, architects exchange CAD files in formats like ArchiCAD or Revit, some 3D BIM files, and lots of sketches illuminated with allusions to Corbu, Aalto and Palladio. Here and now, not at all, only an architecture seen and raw. Projects which, through the diversity of their challenges, tell the story of the strange profession of the Architect who listens, observes, and questions before inventing, forming and awakening.

Images seduce with the light which illuminates them, by their testimony of the rapport between constructed artifact and natural environment or by the sobriety of geometries shaped from wooden walls or plaster as smooth as paper. Strolling while contemplating fabulous bay views through generous windows or nestling in the shade, savoring the pleasures that we draw from space and light is the first step towards architectural desire.

This book is not a museum catalog, however. Each building is the culmination of a unique adventure. This collection of architectural trials ("essais") is an illustrated story of multiple levels of care taken by an architectural firm to respond to the desires and limitations of their clients, while working within technical, economic and social constraints. If you look closely over the course of the projects presented, you will perceive a few themes: the geometric purity of the plan, a geographical specificity, or a programmatic statement that transports us from an abstract academic reading of the design towards intriguing reflections on our relationship to this world of architecture, in which we are continuously immersed.

If these beautiful objects exist before us today, what happened between the initial blank page and the meticulous design of the built project? If perhaps less poetic than the spontaneous generation of an AI arbitrating a statistical median, there is the exciting adventure of discovering needs, necessities and pleasures of spaces manifested in an architectural object.

First there is a physical context with its challenges and opportunities like a rocky ravine in Deer Park, an omnipresent urbanity in 19th Street or a spectacular view in Sugarloaf. This context loaded with its own past destinies appears ambivalent to the modernity that a new buyer wants to bring. The iconic imagery of the Sea Ranch community is filled with the spirit of rusticity and nature into which the Del Mar project inserts equipment made from the most contemporary technologies (radiant floors, solar panels on batteries, smoothed concrete, etc.). Equally radical is the Clay project which, without creating a new floor, simply reshuffles the original 1910 spaces to serve its modern masters. And, not the least important, are the projects filled with humility and respect for the trivial, while subversively reprogramming the formal roots of their spaces, such as the magical dialogue established between the old building and the new of the Tomales project, or the perfect square enthroned on 32nd Ave in the center of Mediterranean architecture from the 1930s in San Francisco.

Sometimes when encountering these natural places steeped in history, improbable functional or spatial qualities emerge, such as the sculptural elegance of the Oak Tree project, built at the counterpoint between a view to the north and solar immersion to the south, or the majestic folding metal roof of Viewcrest which captures rainwater, channels solar flux, and shelters incandescent views with the same alacrity, or the incredible organic insertion of the ribbon wall in the landscape of Anglers Way.

Rather than cataloging design through artificial and formal stylistic tests, these journeys through the projects of DNM Architecture underline the assumed mission of the Architect in the face of complexity. There is evidence of regulatory, technical, and economic complexity, but also a complex understanding of the stakes, social issues, interactions and possibilities. Complexity is finally derived through this duality of aesthetic aporias such as the square and the line as certainties, and the biases of individualized intimacy that each interior space allows us to perceive.

Designing and building spaces that others will inhabit is undoubtedly the dream of those who exercise that vocation, but it is also a serious responsibility, which cannot be executed in the naive innocence of science without conscience! Driving an architectural project to its fruition is a complex mental and physical ordeal which the Architect narrates because it is important that words and objects engage in dialog to create a shared reality. Thus, to accompany these illustrated walks, David Marlatt attempts another exploration of the nature of Architecture through short, precise and fascinating texts. Texts that seem fresh from the latest project, the most contemporary, the strongest, the most intoxicating ... just a little less than the next one that architects aspire to every morning...

Since he has not yet built all his dreams, David speaks to us about architecture as evidence for what may come tomorrow, about the ambivalence of poetic space and of financial cruelty, in which the Architect finds himself obliged to arbitrate between creative insolence and technical pragmatism. To fully explain his role and his work, he strives to show us that he is only the midwife of our own latent ideas, that he helps us to aspire rather than caress our pathological entropy, and that form follows not only function, but also metaphor and analogy. In a way, the Architect explains to us that he is not the despoiler of a blank page, but the inventor of an archeology of our individual knowledge through the means of his own knowledge and experience of geometry, constructive vitality, contextual intelligence, or plate tectonics of cerebral inertia.

There is morality in Architecture and spontaneous power in design. An alchemist's talent, and great cultural and economic wisdom, reside in the architectural studio. In the end, appearances are certainly deceiving, but their discourse is very serious. Architecture is the articulation of this discourse of appearances.

Paris, December 2023

Xavier Soule
Architect DPLG
Doctor in contemporary art history
MST Restoration-Conservation
1st Prize Auguste Perret, 1975
CEO AV Tech Group since 1992

Acknowledgements

David Marlatt, AIA

This book is the product of many people's hard work and dedication, including the dozens of people who worked on these projects while employed at DNM Architecture. In particular, I'd like to recognize the current DNM crew:

- Olivier Pennetier
- Julie Johnson
- Mathilde Manacorda
- Paolo Ciolino
- Alan Marquez
- Karen Eloyan
- Eric Hsu

Successful projects are only possible with successful teams, and I want to acknowledge the many clients who challenged us to think, imagine and implement, and the contractors and engineers who brought our ideas to life.

Special thanks also go to Richard Taylor, who never shied away from big risk and bet on me for my first job out of college (and again and again when I screwed up), and to my friend and former colleague, Xavier Soule, for his kindred spirit and support.

Thanks to the team at Oscar Riera Ojeda Publishers for approaching me with the idea for this book in the first place, and then for their hard work shepherding the idea to reality.

And nothing would be possible or meaningful without my family. Thank you to Jordan, Julien, Justin, and of course… to Sarah.

ESSAYS & ESSAIS

DEER PARK

This project in Marin County, CA, is built on a steeply sloped V-shaped site with a natural drainage swale through its center, effectively dividing the property in half. The site's natural topography simultaneously presented a challenge and an opportunity for a unique building with an amazing view of Mt. Tamalpais and nearby hillsides.

The plan is organized to provide a sense of procession and discovery. Visitors enter the property at one corner and eventually arrive at the opposite, moving from open sky to partially-filtered sky (trellis-covered walkway) to ceiling (indoors) and back out to open sky (patio) – along the way discovering the modern interior spaces and grandiose views.

The design strategy combines practicality and environmental sensitivity to make as little impact on the site as possible. The main dwelling is placed along the slope on the NE side of the lot to minimize grading and maximize the views of Mt. Tam to the southeast. A separate two-car garage and ADU is located on the SW portion of the lot, on the opposite side of the swale, which preserves the natural flow of water through the site. The home's driveway begins near the garage and runs almost flat along the edge of the property (parallel with the road), connecting the two buildings and bringing visitors through the property in a procession of discovery.

Visitors entering the property from the SW corner begin a journey from one corner of the property to the opposite corner. For the first part, they travel by car the length of the driveway, past the garage/ADU building to the entrance of the home. Continuing the journey through the site, a trellis-covered walkway straight ahead brings visitors to the front door and into the home's foyer. A few steps inside, the Living/Dining Room is revealed ahead while large windows over the stairwell draw attention to the natural surroundings below. Continuing into the house, visitors traverse the home and exit to the outdoor terrace and pool where the journey ends in the NE corner of the site.

The house was also designed with efficiency and scenic views in mind. The main artery of the home is the implied hallway that provides the central access point for all areas of the home. The upper level is where most of the daily living takes place.

Once visitors pass through the foyer, a large living room with a 14′ ceiling is revealed. A giant picture window frames Mt. Tam to the southeast and quickly becomes the focal point of the living space. Squared up directly opposite the view is a modern, open kitchen that features custom European cabinetry.

Two large glass pocket doors disappear into the wall behind the fireplace, creating a porous connection to the outdoor terrace, which features living and dining areas, a pool, and dedicated bathroom. The indoor/outdoor relationship between the two living areas, with their shared views and privacy afforded by the site's topography, is California living at its finest.

The primary suite is located on the upper floor and affords the same amazing views from the bedroom and private balcony. The lower level contains offices for the working couple, a family/TV room, and a guest bedroom – for when the grown children visit.

Another unusual feature of this design is its structural steel modular framing, chosen for its durability, fire resistance and weather resistance versus traditional wood framing. Sheathed in stucco and fiber cement siding, the home is hardened against potential wildfire. Additionally, as with all new California homes, there is no gas – all systems are electric.

The structure is highly insulated, and the siting provides minimum glass on the north side and maximum glass on the south with overhangs. The linear design promotes cross ventilation for natural cooling. The home uses a high-efficiency mini split heat pump for HVAC and a high-efficiency hybrid electric heater for hot water. In all, the building exceeds California's T24 energy standards by more than 25%.

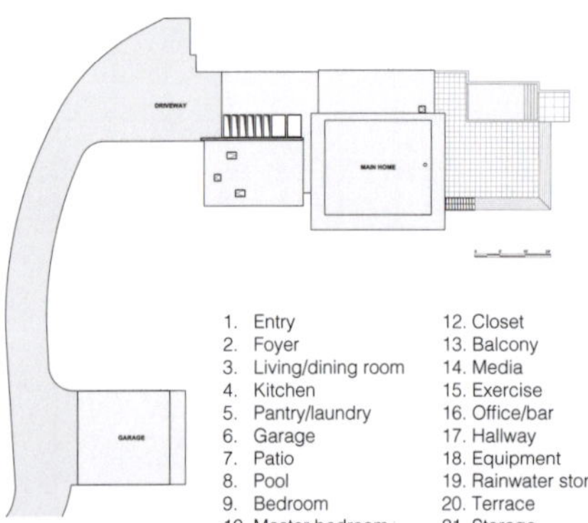

1. Entry
2. Foyer
3. Living/dining room
4. Kitchen
5. Pantry/laundry
6. Garage
7. Patio
8. Pool
9. Bedroom
10. Master bedroom
11. Bathroom
12. Closet
13. Balcony
14. Media
15. Exercise
16. Office/bar
17. Hallway
18. Equipment
19. Rainwater storage
20. Terrace
21. Storage
22. Crawlspace

Site plan

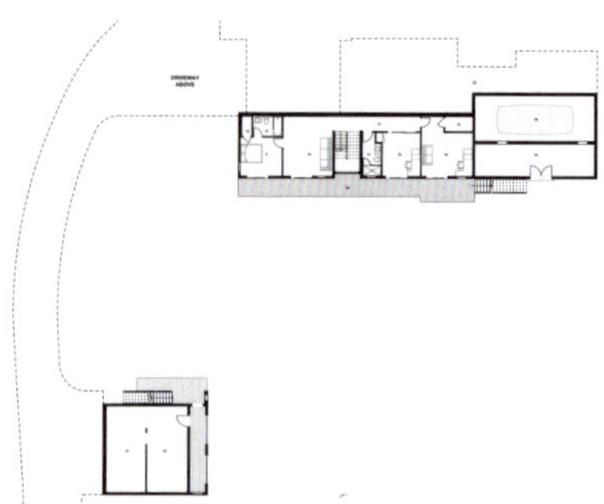

First floor plan

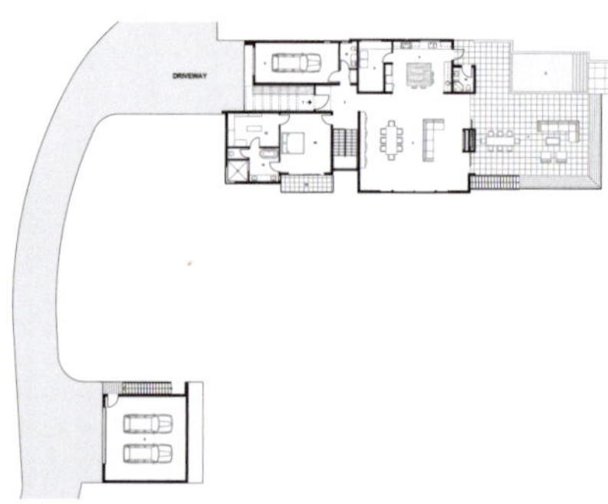

Second floor plan

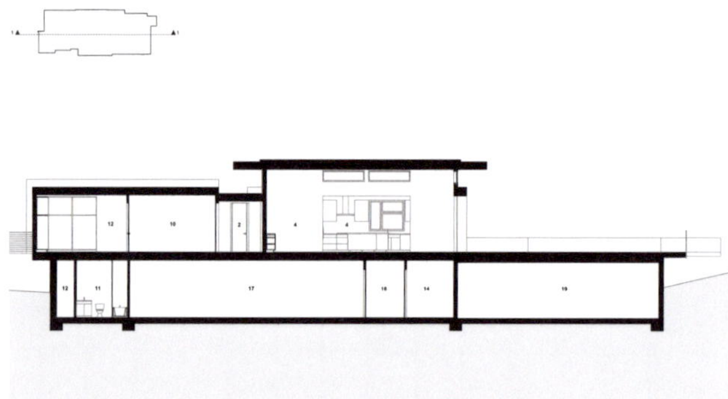

Section 1

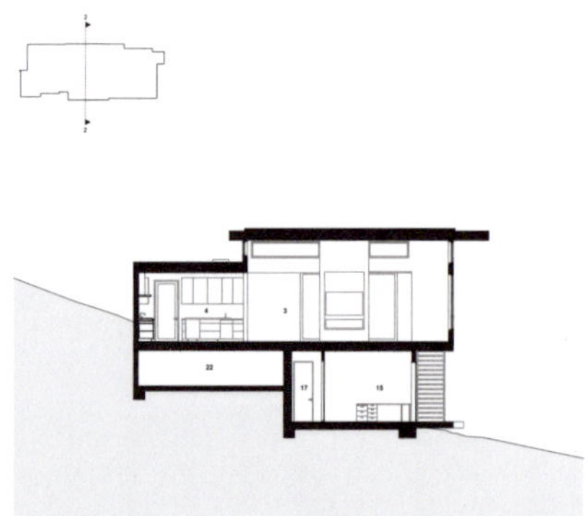

Section 2

Creativity, Beauty and Morality

Creativity, Beauty and Morality are the three standards by which every work of art – including architecture – can be evaluated.

To understand and apply these standards, however, we must understand a basic premise of art: nothing is created from nothing. Every seemingly original work has a context and is derived from some preceding work or works, either as an extension, expansion or a rejection. Artists and architects do not create something from nothing (as Picasso supposedly said, "mediocre artists borrow from others, great artists steal!"). The first law of thermodynamics – that total energy in the universe remains constant even as it is transformed - can be applied to art and architecture. Sometimes literally and sometimes figuratively, artists and architects rearrange the qualities of an existing universe to create fresh objects and expressions. Creativity can be characterized as connecting the same old dots in unforeseen and interesting new patterns. This in no way diminishes the achievements of artists and architects, rather, it reinforces the idea that the potential for art is everywhere among us at all times, waiting to be extracted by the artist's fresh vision of existing parts placed in a new context.

Creativity is a function of Destruction.

Applying the first law of thermodynamics to architecture, there can be no building without destruction whether that destruction is defined as older buildings, trees, ozone, competing ideas, values, preconceptions, potential alternatives, or bank accounts. Every built structure "destroys" the myriad other structures that could have been built on the same site. If creation means a new arrangement of existing parts, the old arrangement must make way for the new. The creative process is necessarily one of erasing and redrawing patterns, tearing down and rebuilding ideas.

When evaluating the creativity of a project, look at what is left in its wake. What has been erased or disrupted by the current work? If the work is a simple derivative of existing patterns (a slightly bigger box, but still the same old box), it may be competent but not very creative. If a work is blindly disruptive, however, it may just be anarchic or ignorant rather than creative. There is nothing especially "creative" about a building with a roof as a floor or no doors and windows or no acknowledgement of the forces of gravity. Such a design is impossible and absurd. It does not disrupt any of our preconceptions and will never be built. When considering creativity, consider the disruption in its wake.

Beauty is a function of Order.

Of all the qualities we may associate with being human, the drive to find the order in chaos, to fight entropy, the tendency of all matter to dissolve into an unordered morass, wherever we encounter it, may be the most uniquely "human." Chaos is unsettling and "ugly." When we sense order, whether in the community, at home or work, listening to jazz or a symphony, looking at Vermeer or Jackson Pollock, we feel satisfied, relieved, calm. We understand. If creativity requires disrupting old patterns to make new objects, beauty requires finding and expressing the inherent order within a set of elements. It might be an obvious static order such as a geometric pattern or an evolving dynamic order like a trigonomic function. It may be asymmetrical but balanced, asynchronous but rhythmic, explosive but comprehensible.

Order only has to reference itself to be successful. Does the work establish an internal logic and follow it? A painting by Salvador Dali or an idiosyncratic house by Bruce Goff establishes its own context and makes sense within that world.

Order can reference external sources, but it must still respect its own internal rules about how to treat the reference. A building may use classical elements in a traditional manner to establish the main entry, express hierarchy or project power. Or it may use those same elements ironically to have us question our preconceptions and see alternative patterns in older buildings. But it cannot do both in the same building at the same time.

Order in architecture can be derived from historical precedent, from other disciplines, from nature, from theory, poetry, or anything else. Order can be regular like a steady drum beat or asynchronous like a jazz ensemble, but it must be intentional. Intention is the hallmark of a coherent order system. It can also be provocative. Sometimes destruction is necessary to clear away obstacles to future expressions of beauty, but there is still order. Robert Venturi and Denise Scott Brown's *Learning From Las Vegas* sought to expose the unexpected order in what was previously overlooked as a banal roadside building. The music of the Sex Pistols might be considered simply destructive (it was intentionally and provocatively not beautiful in any classical sense), but it paved the way for a new musical order of more refined music from REM, Elvis Costello, The Police and others.

An architectural work can be creative and beautiful in a single act by destroying a preconception of a previous order and replacing it with a new order. Frank Gehry's Guggenheim Museum in Bilbao is one example of creating a magnificent cultural destination by replacing the formal preconception of building form with its own rigorous and asynchronous order while simultaneously destroying the cultural preconception of its riverfront site in northern Spain as gritty, industrial and unattractive to tourists.

<u>Morality is a function of Net Gain.</u>

There is no absolute scale that can be applied, but a work of art or architecture should offer a net gain over what was destroyed in its making to be considered "morally good". The simple idea is that buildings that destroy more value than they create are immoral. It's a subjective but straightforward cost/benefit calculation. Fundamentally, we can ask of any work, "Is it worth it?" A new building may be both original and beautiful, but is it better than the previous landmark that it replaced – or the trees and the view? Is the new work worth the loss of longstanding traditions, patterns, communities, and ideas that link present day society to its past? Is it worth the money? Remember that when something is new, something else is lost. The answer to the question, "Is it worth it?" is always subjective and ever-changing, but it must be "yes," for a work to pass from a willful or gratuitous expression to moral designation as art.

The interaction of Creativity, Beauty and Morality can be summarized in three sentences:

<u>Creation without Beauty is anarchy.</u>

When the building or other thing created results only in disorder, it is simply destruction and often a political act rather than an architectural one.

<u>Beauty without destruction is banality.</u>

Banality is often just the blind and uninformed application of old rules to new situations. Nothing is invented and nothing is really disturbed. It is characterized by timidity and conformity. Worse: it is BORING.

<u>Morality without both destruction and beauty is impossible.</u>

A "good" building should be both creative and beautiful. All construction triggers destruction, and creativity is measured as the net benefit of the creation versus the loss of whatever it displaces. Beauty is the revelation of order in creation. Each person will bring their own values and definitions to judging net benefit and order, but they will seek it in any work of art and architecture as the qualities as the bridge between the artifact of art and the expression of their humanity.

DEL MAR

Along the California coast, about 100 miles north of San Francisco, lies The Sea Ranch – a community of homes that exemplifies and preserves the iconic coastal modern architectural style. Established in 1964, The Sea Ranch is based on a simple, enlightened architectural philosophy: each structure in the community should respond to the specific conditions and placement within its environment, but also respond to one another in such a way that they become a cohesive group. Many notable architects of the time contributed to the early residential designs that gave the area its unified architectural style.

The clients are two artists with two grown children. The lot sits at the edge of a giant meadow, nestled against mature Monterey Cypress trees, with common areas and public hiking trails nearby, and a cliffside overlooking the Pacific Ocean just 450 feet away. Among other features, the clients requested individual work studios as well as a vegetable and ornamental garden. The private garden, however, must be hidden from public view to comply with the strict community design standards, which mandate maintaining the Sea Ranch's rustic and natural look.

The architectural concept that developed from the design program is called "The Sun Catcher," alluding to the south facing private garden-courtyard that catches the sun's rays and reflects light and warmth into the living areas of the home. The design is comprised of two separate buildings: an L-shaped main house and a shorter, free-standing garage + office. Together, the buildings frame the hidden sun-catcher courtyard. Both structures are clad in vertical knotty cedar with muted, dark metal window frames to stay true to the area's original 1960s coastal modern design standards. The design makes maximum use of the lot's geographical location and blends perfectly with the community so that to the unaware, it would appear as if it had been standing for decades.

The L-shaped home is oriented to block the strong northwest winds and catch the southern sun reflected from the courtyard. An expansive great room combines the kitchen, living and dining rooms into a public area of the home, and features vaulted ceilings and accordion folding glass doors that open to the courtyard, creating a true indoor/outdoor living experience.

Perpendicular to – and rising above – the living space, the front of the home avoids a clichéd traditional street-facing front door and offers a breezeway with access to the living

First floor plan

1. Motorcourt
2. Garage
3. Trash enclosure
4. Laundry
5. Deck
6. Foyer
7. Bedroom
8. Closet
9. Bath
10. Great room
11. Solar collectors
12. Mech
13. Courtyard
14. Kitchen
15. Studio
16. Breezeway
17. Primary bedroom
18. Primary closet
19. Primary bath

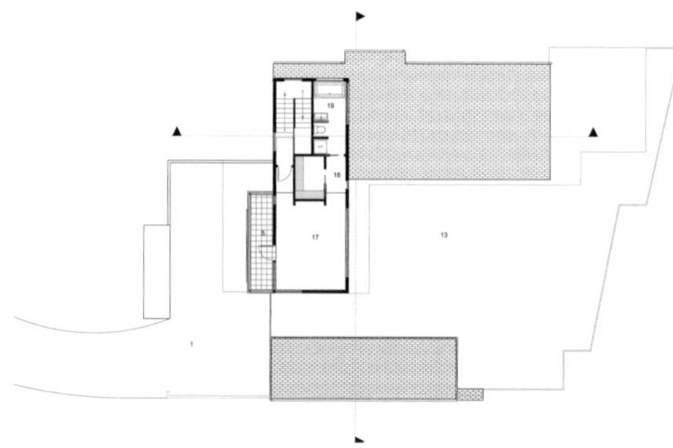

Second floor plan

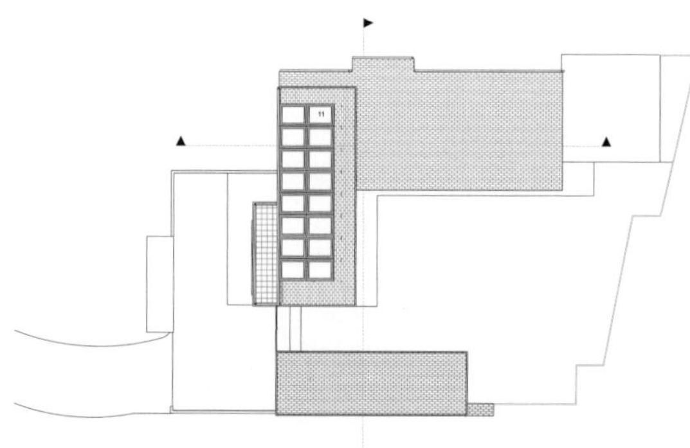

Roof plan

space on the left, an artist's studio to the right, and the courtyard straight ahead. Protecting this entrance is a wooden gate that provides security and a wind screen. Sitting above this front entrance is an expansive primary suite that occupies the entire second floor and features a small deck and corner window where the owners can catch a view of the ocean. This two-story portion is the dominant visual seen from the street.

Lastly, the free-standing garage with attached second studio sits along the southern edge of the lot, providing privacy from nearby neighbors and completing the "Sun Catcher" courtyard.

The house employs innovative heating strategies, including radiant floor heating from electric hot water tanks connected to solar panels and a back-up battery system. There is no gas or propane in the project. Through highly insulated walls and roof, smart geographic orientation, passive design features, and energy efficient appliances and lighting, the home is designed to achieve a net-zero energy use.

1

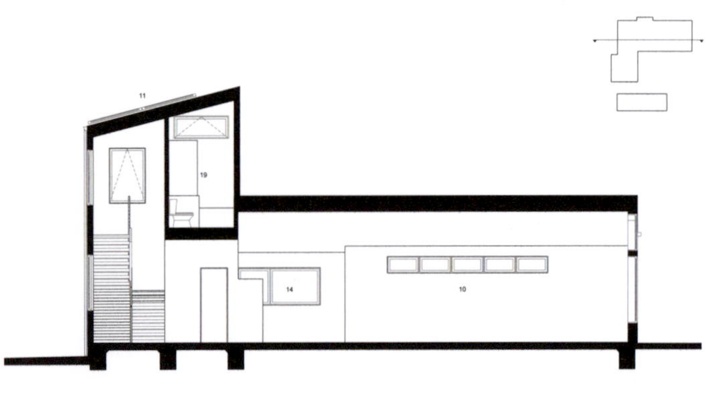

Section 1

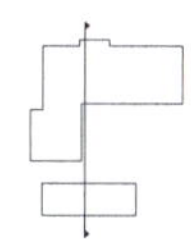

Section 2

19TH STREET

This custom home in an upscale San Francisco neighborhood, built for a technology company executive, fits snugly into its dense urban residential surroundings on a small 24′ x 75′ lot. Completed in 2014, the roughly 25′ square plan contains 3 bedrooms and 2.5 baths in only 1650 sf of living space on three levels plus a two car garage and expansive roof deck with panoramic city views. A second completely remodeled guest cottage on the property completes the two unit compound.

Built on five levels, the house echoes the scale and character of its urban neighbors while maintaining an unabashedly modern and minimalist plan and massing. The north (street facing) facade is composed of glass, wood composite panels and stucco, providing light to the interior and extraordinary city views outward. The south facade faces a small shared yard with the cottage and is composed primarily of translucent insulated polycarbonate panels, a perfect compromise of natural light and privacy. Interior materials are simply white gypsum board walls, dark Oak hardwood floors, white lacquered cabinetry, and neutral limestone tile. A 400sf roof deck with outdoor fireplace and patch of natural planting crowns the structure.

Despite its expansive north-facing orientation, lack of exterior overhangs to the south or other visual clues often associated with "green" homes, this house is USGBC LEED Platinum certified. Its lesson is that energy efficiency and sustainability don't necessarily have to" look" like anything; they are achievable on any site and under any conditions with the right strategies. The north-facing orientation for this house was dictated by the site and tight rear yard setbacks on the south prevented overhangs within the small building envelope. Nevertheless, a number of measures were taken to achieve the Platinum rating target, including careful modeling of cross ventilation through the house, very high efficiency fiberglass doors and windows, a 5-cell-thick translucent R7 insulated polycarbonate panels on the south wall, a high-efficiency hybrid water heater for both radiant heat and domestic use, a heat recovery ventilator to capture and recycle warm air, Energy Star appliances, and many more strategies to reduce waste and maximize recycled content.

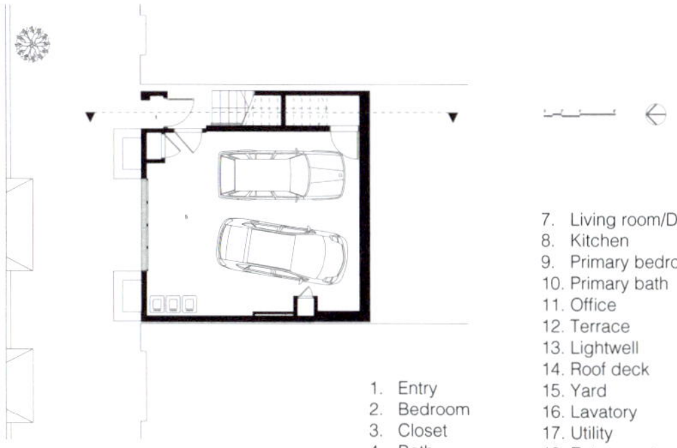

1. Entry
2. Bedroom
3. Closet
4. Bath
5. Garage
6. Cottage

7. Living room/Dining room
8. Kitchen
9. Primary bedroom
10. Primary bath
11. Office
12. Terrace
13. Lightwell
14. Roof deck
15. Yard
16. Lavatory
17. Utility
18. Entry courtyard
19. Solar array
20. Cottage

Garage level plan

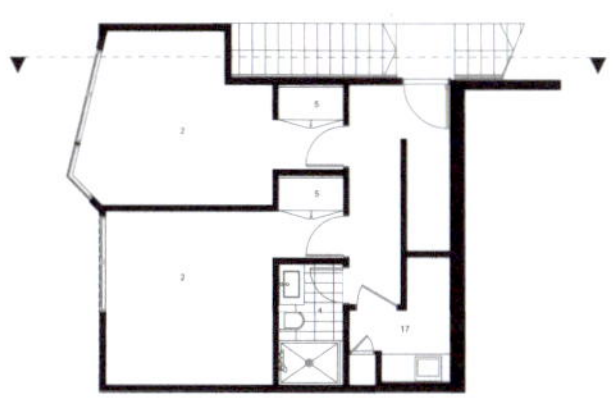

First level plan

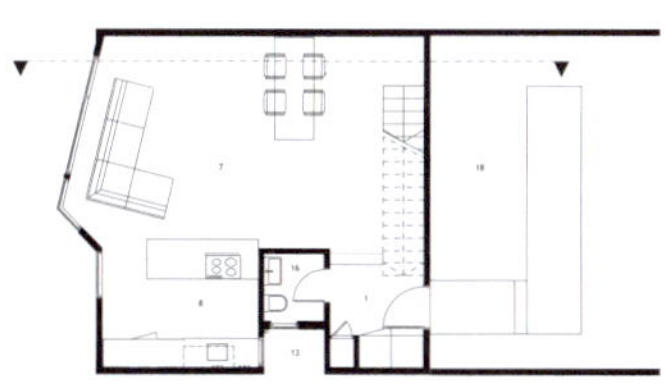

Second level plan

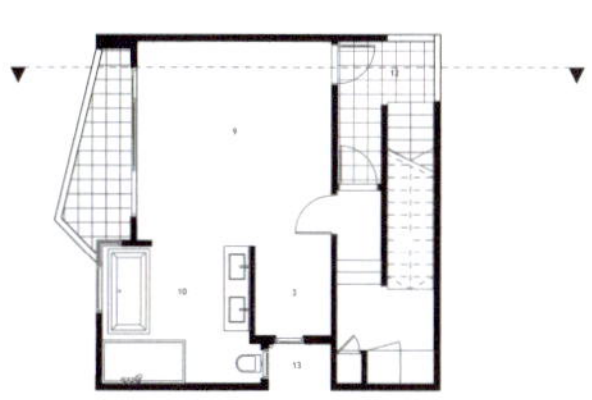

Third level plan

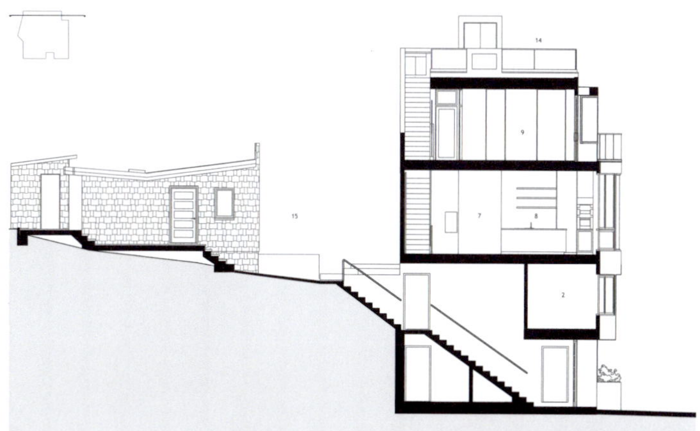

Section

That Building is Alive!

Mark Twain said of his Connecticut home: *"To us, our house was not insentient matter – it had a heart, and a soul, and eyes to see us with; and approvals and solicitudes and deep sympathies; it was of us, and we were in its confidence, and lived in its grace and in the peace of its benediction."*

Personification is a common and powerful way to express our own feelings about buildings. Simple architectural forms – somewhat arbitrarily – are assigned attributes such as strong, feminine, weak, brooding, intelligent, optimistic, and many others. By their association with their builders, architects or physical context, buildings also can be assigned values such as democratic, capitalistic, socialist, even fascist. In his book, *The Architecture of Happiness*, Alain de Botton discusses at length how we can read buildings like we read faces, and how even the subtlest detail or line is noticed and invites interpretation. In order to understand and critique our buildings, we transmogrify cold stone into warm bodies.

There is an inverse corollary to this practice as well. In order to create the architectural designs that will one day be personified themselves, we first turn warm bodies into cold statistics. The real people who will occupy our buildings are reduced to faceless occupants, users, guests, and patients. We know them not by name, but by their demographic profile. Only custom residential architecture is a general exception to this practice of abstracting people into statistics. Custom residential clients retain their actual names, personality character traits, ambiguity, emotions and values.

Long before anything is built, architects often use personification as a design tool. They ask rhetorically what "story" the building might be telling. What does the building "want to be?" Spaces are arranged functionally, but also ceremonially, according to how they might be experienced or "lived," meaning how they might elicit an emotion in the occupant such as wonder, comfort, confidence, pride, intimacy, or even disorientation and anxiety. These are among the many humanistic qualities that we assign to buildings, and which drive spatial organization and form. It may seem that personification is applied to buildings after they are complete, but in fact, the seeds of a building's humanistic traits are planted and cultivated during design.

Why dwell on personification? Because this concept captures a divide in architectural conception between a top-down approach that assumes a given architectural style can be laid upon whatever context it encounters, and a bottom-up approach where building form and style are just the manifestations of humanistic qualities. A top-down approach might be associated with an architect who has a strong style and is hired by the client to deliver a building in that style, more or less independently of the site and client specifics.

A bottom-up design approach prioritizes the occupant's experience(s) over building form. The building's final form is "discovered" or "revealed" rather than imposed by stylistic preconceptions. Adherence to stylistic conventions is not overtly considered. A building's final appearance is a curated manifestation of its design program and their solutions. If a completed building is later classified as "modern" or "contemporary," it is only as a reflection of its contemporary users living in a modern world, with their modern habits, technologies, transportation and norms. Contemporary society is less hierarchical, and relationships are more fluid than they were in past centuries. This logically results in – but does not necessarily require – formal qualities that are associated with modern architecture such as asymmetry, fluidity, and transparency.

Employing personification as an architectural design tool prioritizes procession and how a building or space reveals itself as one moves through it. Personification leverages the idea that buildings tell a story about their occupants and their values and in doing so they engage in a conversation with other buildings and people in the present and future. One can see personification as just a useful device to unlock an architect's creativity, of course, but when a building reflects and embodies the habits, values, and lifestyle of its occupants, it can be experienced as if it is "sentient" (to cite Mark Twain) and a part of the continuous and evolving dialog between people and the buildings that shelter them.

VIEWCREST

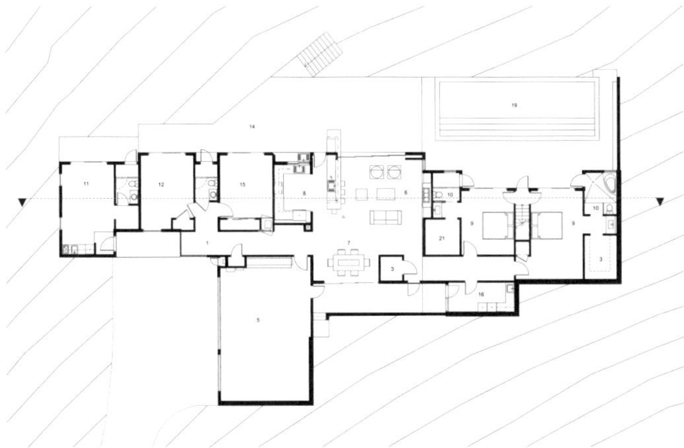

First floor plan

1. Entry
2. Bedroom
3. Closet
4. Bath
5. Garage
6. Living room
7. Dining room
8. Kitchen
9. Primary bedroom
10. Primary bath
11. Studio
12. Hobby
13. Second dwelling unit
14. Deck
15. Exercise
16. Laundry
17. Office
18. Terrace
19. Pool
20. Mechanical room
21. Pantry

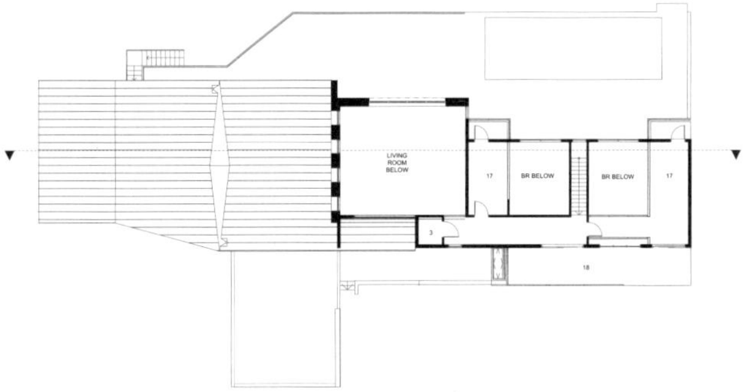

Second floor plan

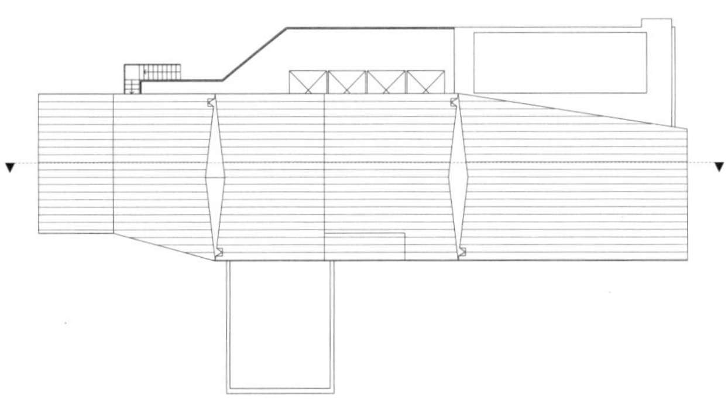

Roof plan

Set against an east-facing hillside overlooking the town of Sonoma, this custom home emphasizes view, ventilation, and controlled solar access. Its orientation towards the panoramic view aligns with the site's natural topography and minimizes excavation and off haul of soil while optimizing cross ventilation. It has been awarded an exceptionally high 180 points in the Green Point Certified House program and employs structural insulated panels (SIPS), insulated concrete forms (ICFs) and other passive and active strategies that minimize energy use. Combined with a 11kwH photovoltaic solar array, the house approaches net-zero energy use. The house also features 20,000-gallon capacity rainwater harvesting that minimizes external water used for irrigation.

Every design decision in the home has multiple purposes affecting function, aesthetics, and livability. The folded roof shape evokes Sonoma County's rolling hills while also maximizing south facing roof surfaces for solar collectors. The plan's shallow depth maximizes both views to the east and cross-ventilation from the reliable afternoon ocean air breezes which roll down the hills from the west. Three-dimensional airflow simulations were analyzed during the design phase and adjustments were made to ensure there were no dead-air spaces. Polished concrete floors provide a modern and zero-maintenance finish as well as thermal mass to modulate temperature swings.

The house also features age-in-place strategies for the retired clients starting with organizing almost the entire house on a single level. The kitchen is split into a "front" and "rear" kitchen that can also accommodate wheelchairs if needed. Two 5' x 5' stacking closets are prepped for a future elevator, and doors are sized to accommodate a wheelchair, if needed. Additionally, an attached studio accessory dwelling unit can be converted into a future care giver's apartment.

The foundations are constructed using insulated concrete forms (ICFs) to temper the crawlspace and minimize heat transfer from above. ICFs also reduce waste by providing formwork for the concrete walls. The building shell is constructed of structural insulated panels (SIPS), which provide a tightly sealed and super insulated shell as well as saving time and labor during framing. The exterior doors and windows are thermally broken aluminum with tinted argon-filled dual glazing. The house is an example of what the architecture critic Charles Jencks once called "multi-valent" design. Its design is derived from balancing the functional needs of the occupants, the formal requirements of energy efficient passive design, and the metaphorical gesture to the rolling Sonoma hills that surround it.

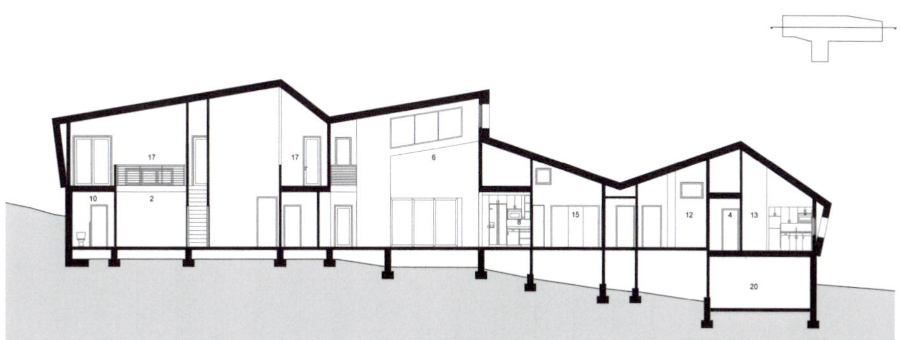

Section

Power of Ten Design

Charles and Ray Eames made a very famous short movie in 1977 called "Powers of Ten." As the camera gains altitude in 10 second increments, it illustrates how perspective and context change algorithmically as we pull back from the immediate object (in this case a picnic blanket), and yet all views are an equally valuable way of viewing the object. Not just picnic blankets, but anything in life can be viewed both up close and from a distance to provide greater perspective and understanding.

Architectural design can be thought of in terms of multiple levels or "altitudes." Up close is the building itself, its walls, roof, doors. Further back is the building's physical context, and further back still – with the building now out of direct sight – might be its symbolic context or the role it plays in the larger society. All of these views are interdependent.

Another way to think about design is in terms of four key characteristics: Aspiration, Context, Practicality and Creativity.

At the highest altitude, a work of architecture is **aspirational**. It hopes to serve some greater purpose than simply providing basic shelter. It might be expressing authority, anchoring a community, conveying warmth, comfort and welcome. Aspiration captures our intrinsic human need at a psychological and sociological level to attach meaning and create order from chaos. We combat entropy in everything we do, and we look for buildings to "make sense" in a larger context, and we assign meanings to them which evolve over time and according to who is using them.

At a somewhat lower altitude, architecture is created within, and shaped by, its context. **Contextual** considerations that impact design are not limited to physical attributes of a site. They include the regulatory context defined by planning and building codes, the financial context that sets the project's market value and budget, and the political context that describes the design review process; the relative power of community members to affect the design through comments and hearings. Political context includes incentives to create new buildings, such as the numerous waivers and other concessions available for Accessory Dwelling Units. And context can include disincentives to building such as historic landmark designations, environmental impact studies, riparian studies and more.

Another few steps closer to earth, **Practical** considerations include all the resources available to build and their respective limitations. Money is almost always the primary practical consideration for any project and a limited resource. However, some buildings depend on donated materials and volunteer labor and their availability and skillsets are practical considerations that impact design. An architect may envision a building in steel when no steel is locally available, and practicality dictates either compromise or opportunity depending on the architect's choices. Younger architects proposing outlandish designs to their bosses frequently use "unobtainium," a miracle material with no practical limitations. Whether guided by money, materials or labor – or all three – if it is true that a design must be constructed to be fully considered as architecture, then practicality is as important as context and aspiration for giving form.

At the metaphorical ground level are **Creative** considerations where everything comes together. This broadly refers to the process of considering aspiration, context and practicality combined with program and function to invent architectural form and space. All are considered simultaneously and without hierarchy. They are just multiple ways to see the same design problem and solution, just as a picnic blanket seen from space is no higher or more important than one seen from the ground. It's only the perspective that has changed.

To mix metaphors further, aspiration, context, practicality, program and function are all ingredients of any design, and the architect applies their own creativity to produce a wonderful and delicious cake. The cake is placed on a picnic blanket which is viewed from ever higher altitudes at the power of ten, and the entire process begins again.

CLAY

Modern living is by no means restricted to single-family homes in the suburbs. The two top floors of this San Francisco condominium were transformed by reclaiming wasted space, opening the floor plan, and adding more windows to capture sunlight and glorious views.

The original Edwardian building was constructed around 1910 as a single-family dwelling and later subdivided into apartments and an ad hoc roof top addition. Already oversized by current zoning standards, no additional area could be constructed.

In the middle of the plan is the central staircase, elevator, foyer, and guest suite. The foyer with its curved wall organizes the plan into public and private space and features a custom-designed shoe bench made of white oak and aluminum.

At the south side of the unit, a new primary suite opens through sliding pocket doors to a new wide terrace carved from the sloped roof and a large primary bathroom with soaking tub and glass-tiled walk-in shower. Skylights are added to extend the southern sun's reach into the rooms, and the space is large enough to accommodate a quiet seating area and fireplace. DNM Architecture designed the bed, end tables, blanket hutch, and dresser. Ash and Walnut woods have been used to create an over scaled box-joint pattern with the drawers and gently curved edges of each piece. Each piece of furniture is a unique piece of art by itself.

Respecting structural walls, the floor plan was opened to maximize views towards the Golden Gate Bridge on the north side. In place of a structural center wall, a series of white oak and walnut display cases conceal columns supporting the roof. The dual-purpose elements showcase the owner's art, while also defining the kitchen space without blocking light as would a solid wall. The new chef's style kitchen is centered around an 11-foot island and is fully outfitted with top of the appliances. Custom cabinetry and millwork in white oak contrast beautifully with the darker walnut floor. The countertops are a flame finished granite, and the backsplashes are contemporary glass tiles.

A DNM-designed circular table made of California Bay wood which can be extended into an elegant oval that seats 10 with a Moooi Heracleum II Chandelier hanging above.

The redesigned living room is organized into two distinctly defined seating areas, one for TV and one for conversation, which take advantage of the glorious, newly exposed views. Thick wood frame windows and a wood-burning fireplace have been replaced by large windows and sliding glass doors that provide unparalleled views of the San Francisco Bay and Golden Gate Bridge. When both sets of doors are open, the indoor/outdoor connection at this elevation – with this view – is inspiring.

In this architecture, the original exterior building features are respected and restored while the new features are contemporary, reflecting both their epoch and the owner's tastes. New and old design features are integrated but remain distinct to express the complete breadth of time from the building's original inception to its current use.

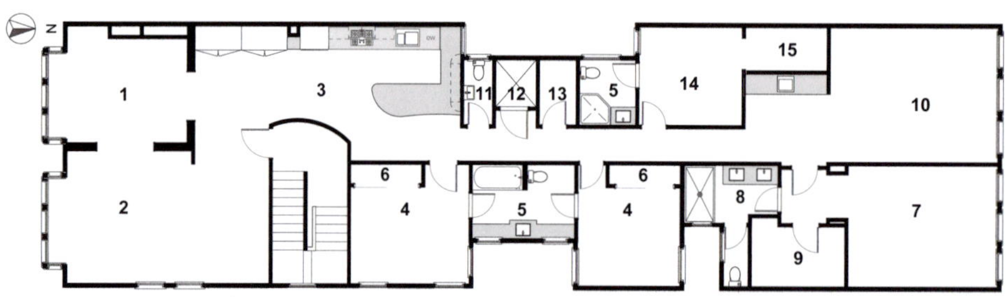

Floor plan

1. Dining room
2. Living room
3. Kitchen
4. Bedroom
5. Bathroom
6. Closet
7. Primary bedroom
8. Primary bathroom
9. Walk in closet
10. Family room
11. Lavatory
12. Elevator
13. Laundry
14. Office
15. Mechanical room

THEO TOBIASSE
PRIMITIVE PAINTING

Tree, Water, Earth and Sky

When starting a new project, facing a blank canvas or a blank computer screen is daunting. Even after analyzing all of the project constraints, where is the starting point to synthesize the information and create something from nothing? This is where literary devices, such as personification, analogy and metaphor, are useful tools to think about architectural design in the context of another medium such as literature, sculpture or, quite often, music (Goethe said "architecture is frozen music").

Architects and all creative professionals use a variety of literary techniques to unleash their creativity and visualize problems in new ways. For example, a building's relationship with its surroundings can be both literal like a slab on grade and metaphorical. A house may be a "tree" that climbs upward to tower over its site or a "boat" floating across the level ground. It may be embedded into the site like an earthen mass, or it may take a blossoming aspirational form that engages the sky.

A house as a tree (as opposed to a treehouse) may have roots in the ground, slender posts or columns and a raised canopy containing living space. There might be a sense of permeability at the ground allowing people to pass among its "trunks." Occupied spaces are elevated, maybe due to a very steep terrain, and their scale is increasingly complex recalling branches and leaves (allusion is another common literary device in the architect's toolbox), as the functional requirements of various spaces are met. The structure is most obviously wood, or maybe steel. It is probably not poured in place concrete.

A house as water implies a broad horizon and flatness. It may be literally over water or just on a level ground plain, maybe on a flood plain. Large expanses of glass may evoke the transparency of water and shimmer in the low sun. It's probably a single level as water does not stack very well. Mies Van der Roe's Farnsworth house may come to mind.

Another meaning for the house as water may be fluidity. A modular house may accommodate a fluid design program by allowing easy additions and modifications. Or, this fluidity may be intended to capture the fungibility of water as in an organically shaped house that follows its terrain along the easiest path.

A house as earth feels like it should be heavily bermed or possibly embedded in a sloped site. Unlike the house as tree, the house as earth hunkers down and cuddles its occupants. We imagine this is due to a harsh environment like the Pueblo villages of the Southwest. Or, it may simply be a lack of building materials as was the case for early settlers in the American Midwest and countless examples of primitive mud and adobe structures. It can be both, of course.

The house as sky implies a structure open to the heavens that compells anyone looking at it to "look up." A dramatic butterfly or other bold roof form may trigger this reflex. The roof is interesting less for its own shape and more for its silhouette. It engages with the sky, and the sky is an essential component of architecture. Looking upward also implies a sense of optimism and perhaps aspiration. Without articulating it as such, we often associate the exuberant architectural forms of mid-century design with a sense of optimism and spirit. When we engage with the sky, we must look up and look outward.

But the house as sky might also be a metaphor for a tower, ascending to the heavens. Metaphors can obviously allude to form as well as function and materials. If expanses of glass close to the ground are "water", perhaps elevated glass or mirrored surfaces can be thought of as "sky." The house of sky may feel ephemeral like a tensile structure.

In architectural design, the "why" informs the "how." Metaphors are just a bridge (hah! another metaphor) joining the two. We use them to help guide our own thinking and our design choices in a consistent, or at least intentional, direction. They are also cultural reference markers for people less familiar with architecture to engage with buildings and understand them in their larger societal context (for example, the virtuous has as a "beacon on a hill"). Architects should think about their work in terms of metaphors but not be enslaved by them, even if these devices don't directly influence design choices. Metaphors are doors that help us let others into our design intent, and they are windows that can show us how others will see our design.

SUGARLOAF

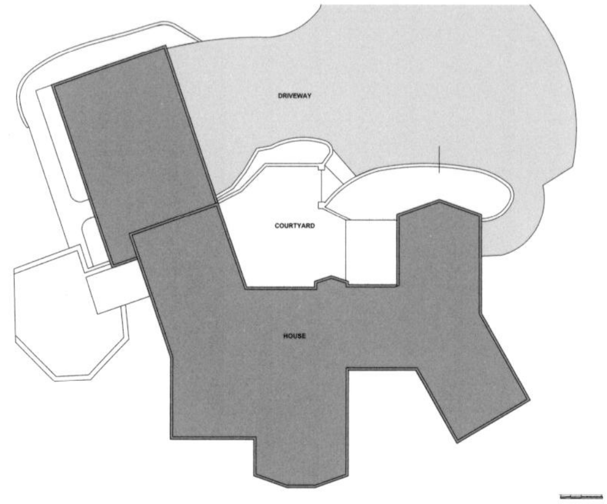

Site plan

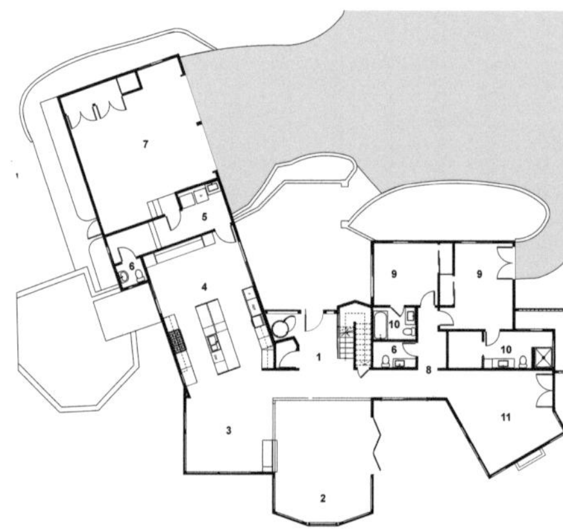

First floor plan

1. Entry
2. Foyer
3. Living
4. Dining
5. Kitchen
6. Laundry
7. Lavatory
8. Garage
9. Hallway
10. Bedroom
11. Bathroom
12. Closet
13. Mechanical room
14. Media
15. Hallway
16. Primary bedroom
17. Primary bathroom

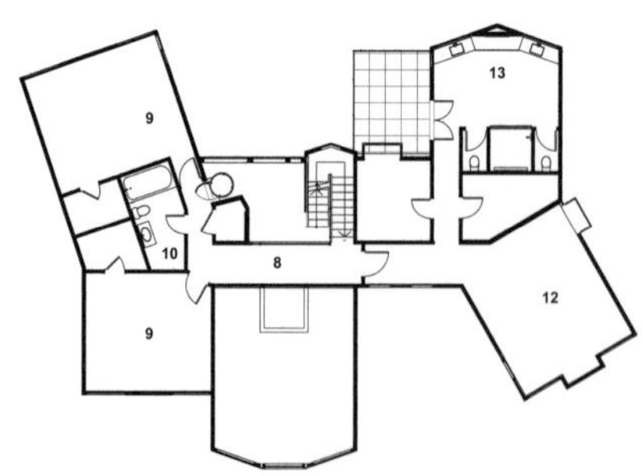

Second floor plan

This reimagining of a mid-century house enjoys 270 degree views from its hilltop perch in Marin County, CA. The original house was a tortured agglomeration of past structures and additions resulting in a second story literally built on the roof of the first story and multiple structural deficiencies. The mission was not just to restore, but to reinvent the home as the modernist architecture to which it aspired.

The plan centers on a new two-story entry that anchors two asymmetrical wings. On axis with the front door and across the small foyer, the view to San Francisco is immediately on display. The view continues as the eye reflexively sweeps right to take in the dining room defined by a peninsula fireplace room divider. The modern kitchen and garage take the reminder of the first story wing. To the left, a hall leads past the staircase to a separate family room and guest rooms. Upstairs, the primary suite occupies one wing while, across a bridge that spans the front entry, two bedrooms and a bathroom complete the other wing. A future pool and detached ADU are planned to complete the composition.

Architecture always tells a story whether intentional or not. This project is the story of a confident and optimistic home, with two wings flanking in a welcoming gesture a core entry and living room. Its large windows frame inspiring views of the San Francisco Bay while generous roofs express both shelter and exuberance.

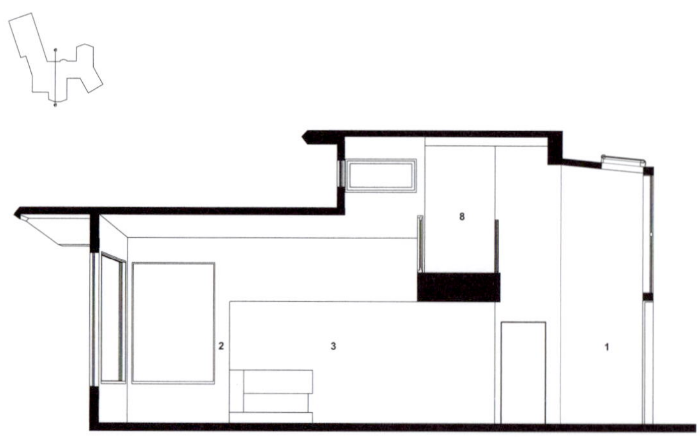

Section

OAK TREE

This three-level family home is embedded in a secluded, north facing hillside with views towards the San Francisco Bay. Its elongated plan follows the site's contours to minimize excavation, and its broad roof tucks under strict town height limits. While the major views from the house are towards the north, the plan also opens south to a courtyard that passively collects sunlight through shaded glass and provides generous cross ventilation and transparency.

The architecture feels sculptural, but every element works to enhance the home's livability and efficiency. A three-story staircase dramatically unites the floors and provides a powerful sculptural element to anchor the courtyard. Expansive decks to the north extend the interior space towards the panoramic Bay view. An imposing two-story "tower" on the southeast corner of the house contains an office and the master bath, but also frames the entrance while shielding private areas from a neighboring house towards the south.

The design exceeds California's Title 24 energy code standards by 26% and achieves 139 points on the Green Point checklist. Broad overhangs and landscaping control shading on the south facade while the house's narrow cross section and openings on north and south sides of living spaces optimize cross ventilation. A high-efficiency boiler coupled with insulated storage tank provides hot water for both radiant heating and domestic use. The house is pre-plumbed for hot water solar collection panels and features a photo-voltaic system on the roof. The house is topped with a standing seam metal roof that is both durable and recyclable.

The house is decidedly modern but draws on familiar domestic architectural cues to announce the point of entry and orient visitors. The home office and primary bathroom form a small tower to anchor the building and articulate the front entrance. A circulation spine, punctuated by a central stair, extends west from the entrance providing access to all spaces to the north and a courtyard carved into the hill to the south. The court becomes another outdoor room, flowing from the family room. To the north, a low-slope roof cantilevers generously over expansive outdoor decks that provide views to the San Francisco Bay.

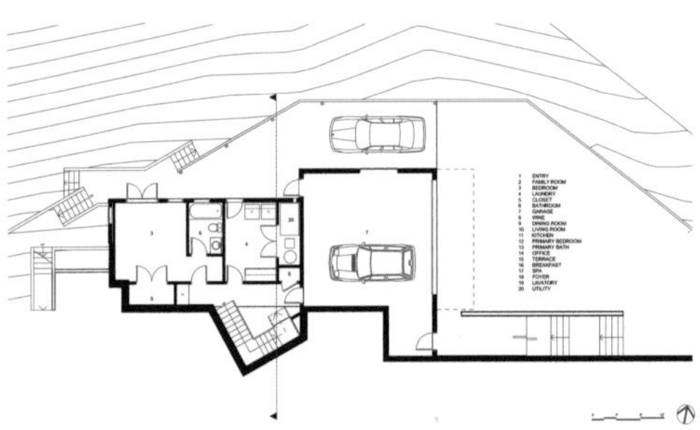

First floor plan

1. Entry
2. Family room
4. Laundry
3. Bedroom
5. Closet
6. Bathroom
7. Garage
8. Wine cellar
9. Dining room
10. Living room
11. Kitchen
12. Primary bedroom
13. Primary bath
14. Office
15. Terrace
16. Breakfast
17. Spa
18. Foyer
19. Lavatory
20. Utility

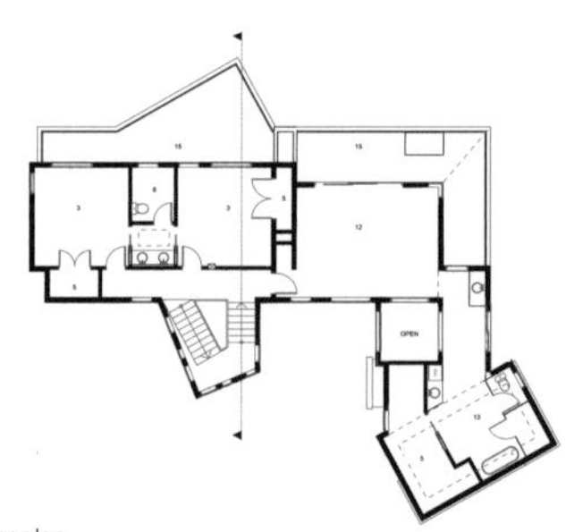

Third floor plan

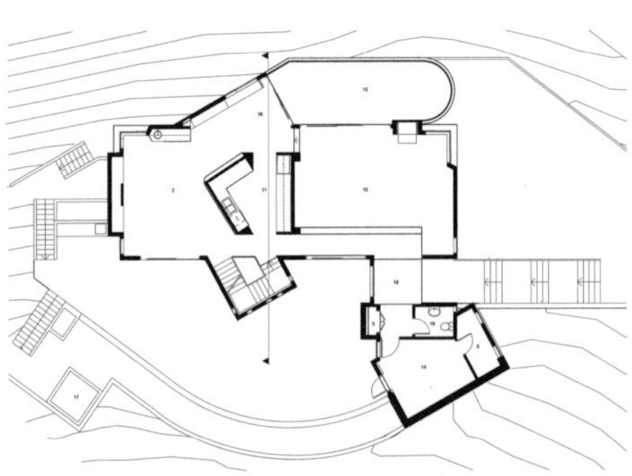

Second floor plan

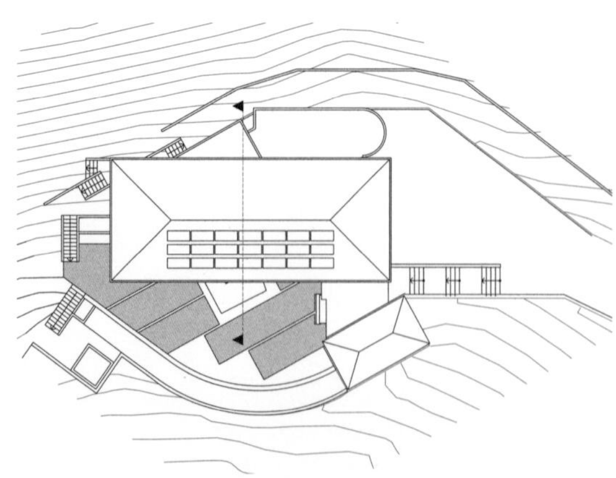

Roof plan

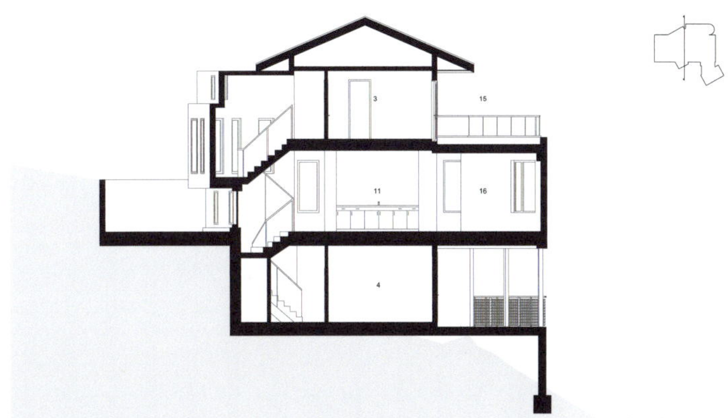

Section

Geometry & Generalist

Architecture is somewhat unique as both a profession and body of knowledge because only architecture approaches societal issues as fundamental problems of geometry. This is not always the best way to approach large problems. Corbusier's Ville Radieuse and later manifestations of public housing such as Pruitt Igoe were failed attempts to address systemic problems of inequity, poverty and racism through site planning and form.

While other professions are responsible for laws, medicines, structures or finance, architects make – or try to make – physical places. Obviously, this approach doesn't solve every problem thrown up against it, but neither does a new law, a new policy, a new derivative, or a new drug. The particular type of three-dimensional thinking that architects embody (this is admittedly a very idealized view of architects), balancing humanism and science, is much more important to society and has far greater practical applications than merely the design and documentation of new buildings across the landscape. Architecture, even when not applied to buildings, represents an alternative way of looking at the world. If architecture as a profession changes fundamentally to the point that it ceases to exist – and we know from history that entire bodies of knowledge can disappear – or if it becomes trivialized until no one appreciates the difference between a making a great place to live and a making a clever teapot, then society will have lost a profound body of knowledge, a portal to solving some of its most entrenched large scale problems using three dimensions, the holistic thinker.

Other professions approach societal challenges as deficiencies in public policy, law, finance, medical diagnosis, or statistics. Industrial and interior designers also bring three dimensional solutions to problems, but those problems almost always exist within an already defined geometric context of rooms, form factors or packaging. Almost unique among professions, architects are fundamentally three-dimensional problem solvers at the scale of buildings and cities.

Moreover, unlike specialized professionals such as structural engineers, mechanical engineers, or geotechnical engineers, an architect is specifically trained to be a generalist, to see both the big picture and oversee the details. There is a saying that an architect knows a little bit about everything, but not much of anything! No other professional on the building project team can talk with about space, light, building codes, history and the strength of concrete with equal ease (and sometimes in the same sentence!). The architect works first with the client to define functional needs, budget, schedule, then analyzes site conditions, building and planning code requirements, and any other external parameters. Then this information is synthesized into an architectural design, and from this creation are derived engineering strategies, material selections and construction methods. All of this under the aegis of the architect in the service of creating a beautiful, strong and functional building or place that successfully resolves the many conditions and criteria that were presented.

You can find architects involved in the design of anything that can benefit from their unique skill set: cities, office towers, hospitals, schools, houses, interiors, furniture, Minecraft, or even dishes. It is the architect's three-dimensional and holistic approach to a design challenge that brings their greatest benefit to society.

ANGLERS WAY

Set on 4.5 acres of rolling pastures in Sonoma County, this two-building composition explores ideas of background/foreground, entry sequence, and arrival. It also explores modern interpretations of traditional rural architypes.

The property at the end of a long narrow private road is entered through a simple gate at the bottom of the site. Glancing upward, a curvilinear cedar-clad wall recalls utilitarian water structures and provides an identifiable landmark for visitors. The wall encloses a one-bedroom 800 square foot guest house, three-car garage, and music studio.

The driveway ascends past this curvilinear structure to reveal the orthogonal forms of the main house poised above. The exterior materials are an earth-toned palette combining natural cedar siding, warm white stucco, and dark galvanized metal for windows, doors and deck railings.

The driveway continues its winding ascent past a grove of olive trees to a motor court near the top of the site. Exiting their automobile, visitors climb a final exterior staircase along the east facade to the sheltered front door with dramatic views back down the hill to the pastures beyond. Entering the foyer in the middle of the plan, the family area of primary suite and office are zoned to the right and public spaces to the left. Entering the living room with its 14' ceiling, the panorama to the south and east explodes into view, and a second floor terrace wraps the southern and eastern facades, inviting views and connecting the house to its sloped site.

The ground floor contains a private two-bedroom apartment with its own expansive shaded terraces and a three-car garage. A home elevator connects the two levels as part of the home's age-in-place strategy.

Energy efficiency is also of paramount importance with high efficiency heating and cooling systems, heavily insulated walls and roofs, overhangs carefully calculated to optimize shading and solar collection, cross ventilation, EV chargers, and more than 10KwH of photo-voltaic panels.

In some respects, the project harkens back to a time of landed estates with multiple structures, controlled approach, and even a small vineyard. It offers private living, but also very public spaces for receiving and entertaining visitors. Reflecting the values and lifestyle of its occupants, however, its architectural vocabulary is contemporary, low maintenance and practical. Like the simple utilitarian rural buildings that it seeks to emulate, the home design is a direct expression of its functional and symbolic design program.

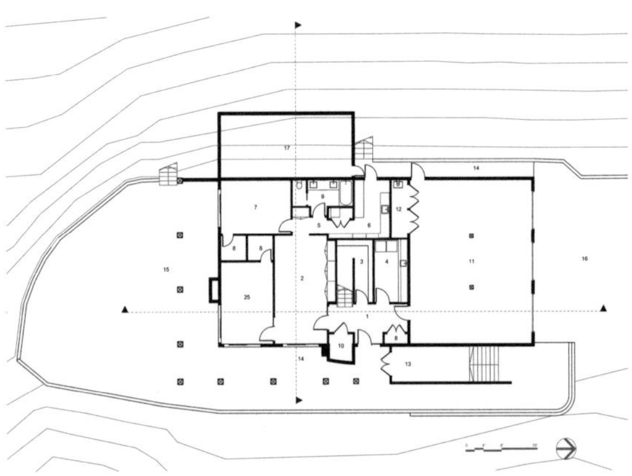

First floor plan

1. Entry
2. Family room
3. Wine cellar
4. Laundry
5. Hall
6. Utility
7. Bedroom
8. Closet
9. Bath
10. Elevator
11. Garage
12. Mech
13. Storage/garbage
14. Walkway
15. Terrace
16. Motorcourt
17. Crawlspace
18. Living room
19. Dining room
20. Kitchen
21. Back kitchen
22. Bar
23. Primary bedroom
24. Primary bath
25. Study
26. Lavatory
27. Deck

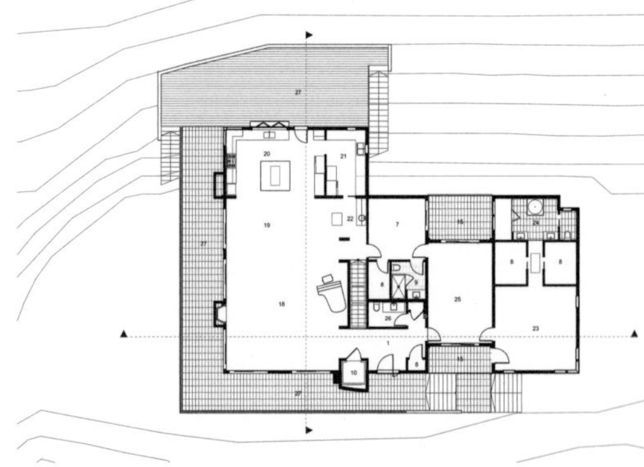

Second floor plan

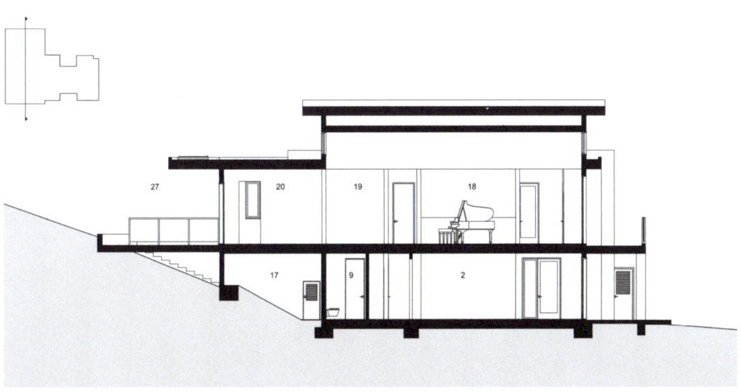

Section 1

Section 2

Building is a War Against Inertia

While listening politely to neighbor concerns in a planning commission meeting (all valid, if not necessarily relevant to the project at hand), or while debating over building code minutiae with a building department plan checker, or while filtering all of the reasons from a general contractor that a building is simply *impossible* (unless they are hired, of course), I find my mind returning again and again to the same theme: building is an act of war against inertia. Any change, physical, spiritual, or otherwise, requires effort, and effort is another way of expressing energy. Building anything requires a great deal of effort and energy to alter the physical, financial, political, and even cultural status quo.

There can be no construction without destruction. The simple act of building anything destroys or at least displaces whatever else that was occupying that space previously. At a tangible physical level, dirt is dug, plants are removed, trees are often cut, and possibly older structures are demolished. This type of destruction meets resistance from the defenders of dirt, grass, trees, and older structures. But other things are also destroyed or altered by the act of building, and this can be less obvious, such as the client's bank account balance that is exhausted when funds are displaced to pay for the project and are no longer available for other potential projects which now will never be realized. The destroyed things can be completely intangible and abstract, such as when a client's abstract dreams for a hundred alternative new houses are consolidated into a single artifact that will become the actual new house in which he or she will live. When one house is built, all of design alternatives are extinguished with all of their unrealized potential. The act of building, with its need for financing and concrete decisions, leaves in its wake the debris of all other potential dreams and projects for which those funds and those decisions and that energy might have been spent. It is little wonder that any building project, no matter how merited, meets resistance, sometimes active, and sometimes just procrastination. Building is not just the act of making something; it is also the act of giving up what might have been.

Understanding that making something means giving up something else, the reality that all projects meet a wall of inertia is understandable. And, like every natural force, inertia acts equally on all that it encounters. It is neither good nor bad. Inertia's greatest manifestation in society is government bureaucracy. Bureaucracy inherently slows and resists change while ostensibly facilitating it, but that's not necessarily a bad thing. With equal disregard for all it encounters, institutional bureaucracy can slow down a bad idea until a better idea comes along just as easily as it can slow down a really good idea until it loses the energy to move forward and dies on the vine. As Isaac Newton first formulated, overcoming inertia requires effort. "Effort" can be in the form of the physical effort to move dirt and lift steel in the air, but it can also be the effort to overcome cultural and legal hurdles, secure financing, and manage complex and protracted approval processes. Effort can be measured in tons and cubic yards or in the months, years and dollars required to overcome political, cultural and financial obstacles.

Before drawing swords against inertia that slows projects, however, let's also recognize that inertia (in reasonable doses) is essential in a democratic society. It slows down ill-conceived projects and ensures that there is time for a deliberative process that considers multiple views and compromise. Without sufficient time to deliberate, a community's voice cannot be heard and it will feel – and sometimes it will be in fact – steamrolled by a developer's juggernaut and the cash-strapped government that permitted it. Although everyone wants progress (or says that they do), no one wants to make mistakes that will rest in the landscape for generations. A little bit of judicious inertia is most often a very good thing.

Caught between a desire to do good and a duty to serve their client, an architect is tempted to seek a compromise between the inertial forces gathered against construction and the destructive forces necessary to build. Resistance to change is often institutionalized and somewhat faceless such as a building department, a bank, or a neighborhood group. And it is probably well-intentioned, trying to preserve something it regards as more valuable than the building being proposed, such as money, other buildings, neighborhood patterns, or trees. Indeed, architects must be patient with, and even empathize with, the very people that often slow them down. As licensed professionals, architects have both legal and ethical duties to public health, safety and welfare that transcend their immediate design problems.

But a work of architecture must be built to be complete, and it is the architect's professional duty to shepherd their client's projects to successful completion. Any architect with an active project is a change agent and therefore – always, unavoidably, and inevitably – an adversary of the forces of inertia aligned to stop or slow their project. Governments speak for their electorate. Banks speak for their investors and capital. Neighborhood groups speak for their communities. Architects speak for their buildings. It's their job.

Building may not be the equivalent of waging war, but it is at least a struggle balancing the priorities and exigencies – often contradictory – of multiple parties. And while architects may only stand one side of the struggle (i.e. be pro-building), they also know that the creative forces driving change are just the Ying to the Yang of the inertial forces that slow them down. Speaking at a design commission hearing, sifting through a contractor's list of reasons they deserve more to do less, listening to a client's accountant explain why the project "just doesn't pencil," the project's seeming adversaries are playing an essential role making the final project stronger in ways that the architect doesn't fully control. The architect is the advocate of the building, and the inertial forces that may appear opposed to building are also doing their job to help insure that what is being created will be of greater value than all of the trees, grass, money, dreams and parallel possibilities being displaced.

TOMALES

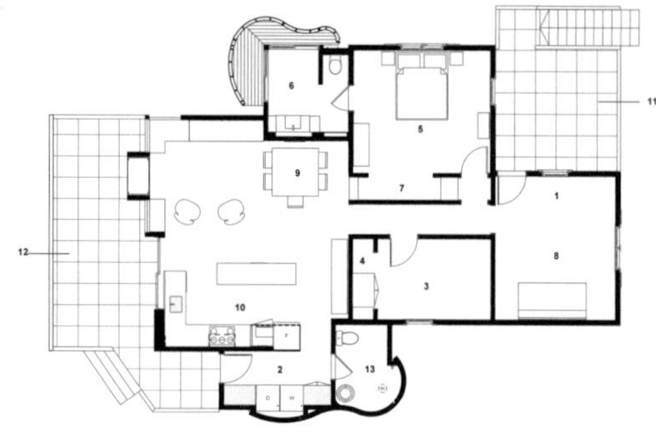

Upper floor plan

1. Entry
2. Laundry
3. Bedroom
4. Closet
5. Primary bedroom
6. Primary bathroom
7. Primary closet
8. Living area
9. Dining area
10. Kitchen
11. Deck
12. Porch
13. Bathroom
14. Studio
15. Unfinished basement
16. Garage

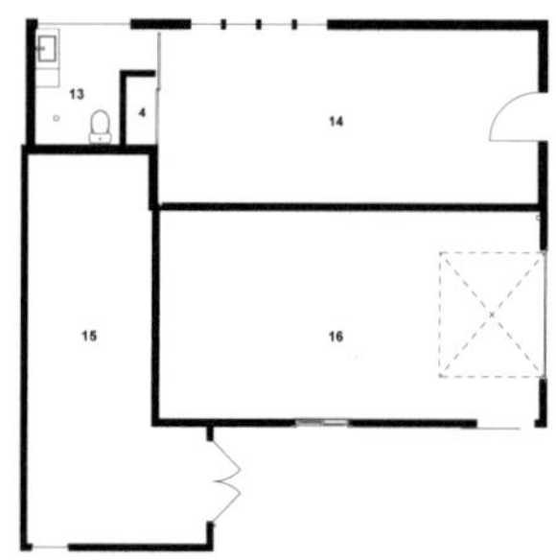

Lower floor plan

Situated in Marin County, north of San Francisco, the original home, framed and clad in Redwood, dates from 1906 and was originally sited on hillside land closer to Richardson Bay. The US Army arrived in 1942 to create the vast Marin Shipyards, consuming entire neighborhoods, and the original house was moved to its current corner lot in a quaint neighborhood in Sausalito.

Consuming just 875 square feet when purchased by the current owners, all of the living spaces were on one floor above a single-car garage and an unused crawl space. The first phase of the renovation removed cheap wallboard, carpet and other finishes installed by an egregious landlord. The original Redwood tongue and groove paneling was exposed and finished in white. Lighting was updated, and a new hardwood floor was installed on top of an earlier vinyl floor.

During the second phase, the entire crawlspace area under the home was excavated for a new 400 square foot guest studio and full bathroom that provides added living space and seismically upgraded foundations to match the original design. For the privacy of both homeowner and guests, the new space has its own front entry and no internal stairs.

Phase 3 of the serial remodel included a new primary bathroom featuring a perforated aluminum privacy screen to protect an open shower and private garden. A new standing seam metal roof replaced the shingle roof and provided rigid insulation. Solar panels were added.

The final and largest phase removed the two porch extensions and added a contemporary kitchen/dining/family room, laundry and additional bathroom on the east side, wrapped in perforated metal. A gentle counterpoint to the white-clad original cottage, the new space opens to the rear yard with expansive glass, a pocket sliding door and see-through fireplace. Clad in blackened Cedar boards to contrast with the white cottage, the new addition's roof slopes slightly upward towards the southwest-facing backyard to expand the view and capture the sun as well as channel rainwater to a 750-gallon tank in the basement where is used for landscape irrigation.

Each expressing domestic shapes and materials in its own manner, the addition and the cottage are engaged in a polite dialog between old and new, retaining their respective identities and reflecting their epoch. History is respected but not mimicked, all the better to appreciate it. The new parts of the house are expressed as such, and their design represents the current lifestyles and needs of their occupants. The renovated house metaphorically lives in its modern world while retaining its roots in the past.

TOMALES

CAMPING

LA MINUTE DE VERITE

ORDRE
MOBILISATION GENERALE

Finding a Way Forward

A popular book on evolution from some years ago, *Climbing Mount Improbable*, by Richard Dawkins, explains that extremely complex organisms and assemblies evolve through extremely slow and tedious baby steps, climbing the "gentle slope" of evolution. No miracles or giant leaps are required much less permitted. Each baby step of evolution from protoplasmic organism to modern humanity must be an improvement on the previous step – and must deliver an immediate benefit – or it simply will not occur. In the clear and brutal logic of evolutionary theory, this is because an organism that incorporates any change from its predecessor or its neighbor a) will have no motivation to make that step unless there is an immediate benefit and b) will die before creating offspring that will also incorporate that step if there is no immediate benefit.

As a result of this extremely short-sighted behavior by organisms to selfishly think only of their survival, they can never reverse their evolutionary progress, even temporarily, even if it is obvious to higher organisms such as ourselves or Richard Dawkins that they have headed down an evolutionary dead end. That is, they can never descend the evolutionary slope they are on so that they can begin climbing another more promising hill that may take them even higher. Put another way: in the gearbox of evolution there is no reverse. An organism cannot back down an evolutionary road that appears to be a dead end so that it can take another fork in the road. It can only find its way out of a mess by moving forward or it can stall and cease to evolve further.

This predicament – trapped in a dead end or as Dawkins says, stranded on a hillock in the foothills of Mt. Improbable – can be relieved in just a few ways. First, circumstances may change in a way that alters the "landscape" and opens new evolutionary paths. For example, global climate change such as an ice age might "suddenly" favor an animal with heavier fur and slower eating habits over a lighter animal with no fur that needs to forage constantly. Secondly, attributes from another stranded organism on a faraway hill might travel (by wind or bees or birds) to cross pollinate with other organisms and contribute new attributes that the first organism needs to advance on the evolutionary ladder. Lastly, and most rarely, a sudden change or gross mutation – effectively a miracle – can yield a sudden positive change and help the organism leap forward. This third option is extremely rare because the odds of any sudden change yielding a positive effect are remote. As Dawkins says, there are many ways for an organism to live, but there are many more ways for it to die.

You might now be wondering if this relates to the architectural profession and building industry (or the analogy of painstaking slow incremental change may already be all too obvious). Having already read this far, you can't just "unread" what you have read. You can certainly abandon it and move to other activities, but you can't really go backwards. Welcome to evolution.

Applying this Darwinian concept to some Internet-based businesses in the recent past, we can understand their successes and failures much better. So many of them just assumed that customers would see the long term benefit of using their platforms and they would make a collective short term sacrifice – essentially move backwards from what they were currently doing – to achieve it. Many companies based their entire business on the belief that all of their customers would somehow reformat their own business to a common new business format that would eventually benefit everyone. The key word is "eventually" and the fundamental flaw was that their customers were also competitors with each other. They did not last

One large and unsuccessful start-up in the early 2000s had the ambition (and the investor list) to transform the entire residential construction industry in a single mighty transformational blow by buying up all of the small accounting software and related vendors they could and moving everyone to a great unified industry standard for the procurement and distribution of building materials. In hindsight, it is amazing that so many really smart people could be hypnotized so well for so long and came so close to a suicide leap into the precipice between their little hill of inefficiency and the shining mountain of industry wide supply chain efficiency that was promised. They were selling a vision of a promised land on a high distant mountain in the Mt. Improbable Range, but getting there was predicated on not just one company, but ALL companies in the building industry simultaneously taking a giant step down their own slope and somehow walking up together to this new promised land. Despite significant investment from most of the major US home builders and other institutions, this move simply defied the fundamental laws of evolution, and the entire effort ultimately failed spectacularly. Years later, the building industry has improved slowly and incrementally, but still sits today on its innumerable, inefficient, infighting, little hillocks while the higher mountains populated by so many more efficient industries such as financial services, aeronautics, automobiles or information technology, look down with bewilderment.

Successful companies moved in slower, and always positive, increments. Some started delivering movies on DVDs before evolving to online delivery and ultimately producing music for the content they distribute. Another pretty obvious example started selling just books, then selling everything, then warehousing and delivering everything, then adding services to the stuff it sells. For the customer, no single step is backwards. Benefit is layered upon benefit which is layered on benefit.

If not already clear, the message is that no matter how obvious might be the faults of any industry, and no matter how obvious might be the advantages of adopting better systems, better organization, better efficiency, etc. enjoyed by others, the industry (or the "market," customer, and anyone who might be considered part of the industry) cannot walk backwards – cannot intentionally go downhill – to take a different course that may eventually lead to a higher ground. Forward is the only way to go and each incremental step must be self-sufficient. Each step must pay its own way. If any step even temporarily disadvantages any player in the industry, be it a professional sacrificing proprietary information, a government agency sacrificing control, a customer sacrificing purchasing power, a supplier sacrificing delivery times, or contractor sacrificing a competitive advantage, that player would essentially be agreeing to take a bullet for the others. This is very rarely how society works and certainly not the way that business is expected to work. In a public company, such an intentional short term disadvantage might even expose its management to lawsuits if they are suspected of operating even briefly against the shareholders' interests.

Although it is widely accepted that it is still fractured and highly inefficient, the construction industry has so far resisted most fundamental change that might improve efficiency, reduce material waste and delivery times, and speed construction precisely because no company has come up with an incremental forward moving path towards achieving change. No one with any industry knowledge would dispute the handicaps suffered by the building industry as it is currently organized, which range from a highly fractured design profession, antiquated models of government oversight, cultural biases by both builders and clients, deplorable supply chain management, and rampant lack of technology standardization. Most proposed solutions, however, require sacrifice, re-tooling of processes, sharing of confidential information, or adherence to complex and simplistic CAD formats. Innovators mistakenly think that change must be quick to take hold; in fact, it can be slow (or quick) as long as it is positive. In other words, no one has yet found or invented the magic map that can lead the industry to higher ground without reversing its course or going downhill.

So, for lack of a path forward from their various hilltop fiefdoms, the major players in the building industry wait for change from cross-pollination: radical, game changing ideas with game changing acronyms like BIM, IFC, IPD, LEAN, TQM, and others, that will propel their own company to new levels, and pull the rest of the industry along in their wake. They will be waiting a long time… While, indeed the building industry is more efficient than ten years ago (largely due to improvements in online services during the pandemic), nothing has fundamentally changed the design/permit/construction paradigm and the efficiency gains are mainly the side effects of general improvements in online publishing, web-based procurement, video conferencing, GIS services, and shipment tracking rather than any "homegrown" building-specific solutions.

The construction industry and the architectural profession are changing in small positive steps. The worldwide exigencies of climate change, a chronic housing shortage, wealth inequity, mass migration due to weather events and war, and other challenges force the question whether slow evolutionary steps can be enough. Richard Dawkins described three ways that evolutionary change occurs: incremental positive steps, cross pollination of ideas from other industries, and lastly, miracles. Cross pollination is happening, some government agencies are learning to streamline, newer lower carbon building materials and techniques like 3D printing are on the horizon. Let's hope we don't rely on miracles.

32ND AVENUE

Viewed from the street, this house is a traditional and pristine home in one of San Francisco's western neighborhoods that slope gently to the ocean. Inside, however, unfolds a surprisingly open, eclectic, contemporary, and family-friendly design on three levels. The design melds inventive artistic features with classic elements of a 1931 California Mediterranean house. It is a dialogue between the past and an evolving present.

A small interior lightwell yields to a new staircase with a gently angled wall that yields headroom. The remodeled kitchen re-uses the home's original cabinetry and is united by a sinuous poured-in-place concrete countertop with a cylindrical sink made from a restaurant grade pasta bowl allowing 270 degrees of access. While the style reflects artistry, the design is always functional.

A sunny breakfast room features a hand painted ceiling by the artist-owner and a suspended light made from a colander.

Passing through the living room to the perfectly square skylit dining room in the center of the plan reveals a staircase inserted into a former lightwell that connects the upper and lower levels. The dining room features another whimsical light fixture composed of copper plumbing pipe and cages meant for candles.

Beyond the kitchen and dining room, the rear of the house is zoned for private use with four bedrooms and two bathrooms. A dramatic bathroom is a composition of slate and mirror with a transparent counter and an open shower. Two bedrooms complete the second floor plan while a sculptural Oak and Fir ship's ladder leads to a sunny loft with a finished skewed plywood ceiling.

The original Douglas fir floor framing below is cleaned and neatly exposed downstairs, where there is a primary suite and small office separated by simple barn doors of OSB. Down the open stairway from the main level with its gently sloped wall yielding headroom, is a media room and the primary bedroom, both drawing light from the garden through a glass wall. The ceiling exposes the house's original Douglas fir floor joists and subfloor, cleaned and carefully devoid of unsightly wiring or plumbing. Form fuses with function with sliding privacy walls of simple OSB, stained concrete floors, and Japanese Tansu-like cabinetry integrated into the staircase. The colorful Moroccan inspired sky-lit primary bath reveals an oversized soaking tub.

In addition to numerous alterations and upgrades made over time, insulation was added throughout the house and a photo-voltaic array installed.

The home is an ongoing conversation between its restored past and evolving current occupants. Old is honored and new is expressed in an often idiosyncratic and whimsical manner that emphasizes humanity over formal composition.

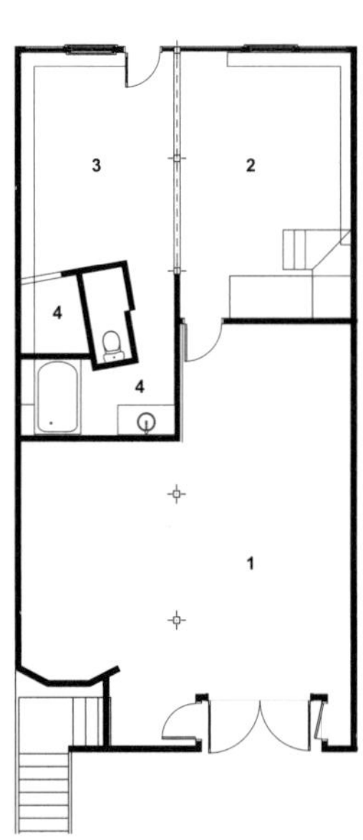

First floor plan

1. Garage
2. Office
3. Bedroom
4. Bathroom
5. Closet
6. Kitchen
7. Dining room
8. Living room
9. Breakfast room

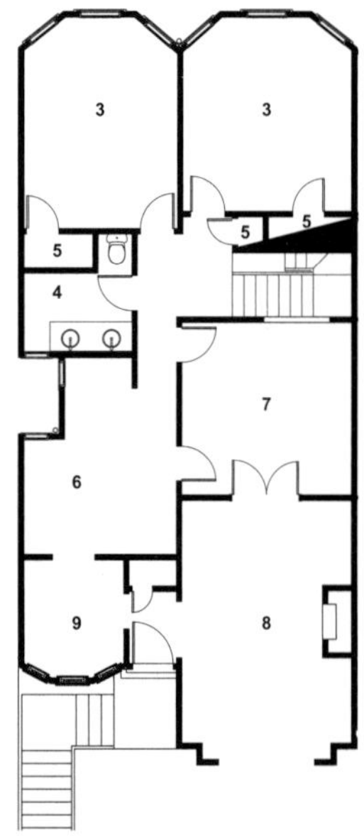

Second floor plan

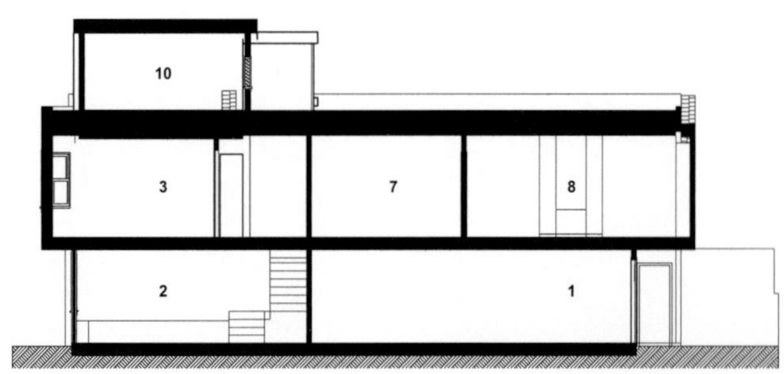

Section

Viewed from the street, this house is a traditional and pristine home in one of San Francisco's western neighborhoods that slope gently to the ocean. Inside, however, unfolds a surprisingly open, eclectic, contemporary, and family-friendly design on three levels. The design melds inventive artistic features with classic elements of a 1931 California Mediterranean house. It is a dialogue between the past and an evolving present.

A small interior lightwell yields to a new staircase with a gently angled wall that yields headroom. The remodeled kitchen re-uses the home's original cabinetry and is united by a sinuous poured-in-place concrete countertop with a cylindrical sink made from a restaurant grade pasta bowl allowing 270 degrees of access. While the style reflects artistry, the design is always functional.

A sunny breakfast room features a hand painted ceiling by the artist-owner and a suspended light made from a colander.

Passing through the living room to the perfectly square sky-lit dining room in the center of the plan reveals a staircase inserted into a former lightwell that connects the upper and lower levels. The dining room features another whimsical light fixture composed of copper plumbing pipe and cages meant for candles.

Beyond the kitchen and dining room, the rear of the house is zoned for private use with four bedrooms and two bathrooms. A dramatic bathroom is a composition of slate and mirror with a transparent counter and an open shower. Two bedrooms complete the second floor plan while a sculptural Oak and Fir ship's ladder leads to a sunny loft with a finished skewed plywood ceiling.

The original Douglas fir floor framing below is cleaned and neatly exposed downstairs, where there is a primary suite and small office separated by simple barn doors of OSB. Down the open stairway from the main level with its gently sloped wall yielding headroom, is a media room and the primary bedroom, both drawing light from the garden through a glass wall. The ceiling exposes the house's original Douglas fir floor joists and subfloor, cleaned and carefully devoid of unsightly wiring or plumbing. Form fuses with function with sliding privacy walls of simple OSB, stained concrete floors, and Japanese Tansu-like cabinetry integrated into the staircase. The colorful Moroccan inspired sky-lit primary bath reveals an oversized soaking tub.

In addition to numerous alterations and upgrades made over time, insulation was added throughout the house and a photo-voltaic array installed.

The home is an ongoing conversation between its restored past and evolving current occupants. Old is honored and new is expressed in an often idiosyncratic and whimsical manner that emphasizes humanity over formal composition.

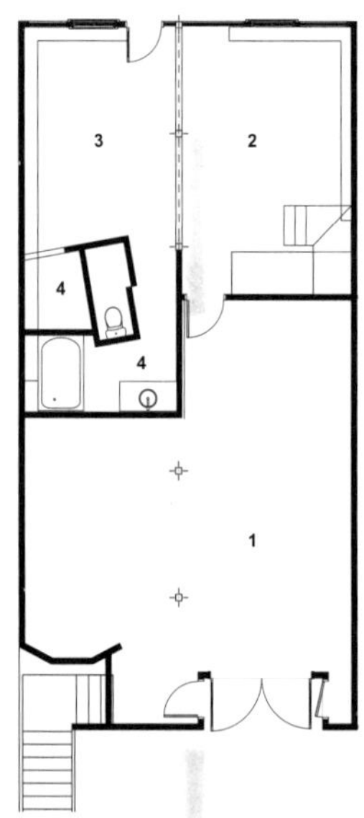

First floor plan

1. Garage
2. Office
3. Bedroom
4. Bathroom
5. Closet
6. Kitchen
7. Dining room
8. Living room
9. Breakfast room

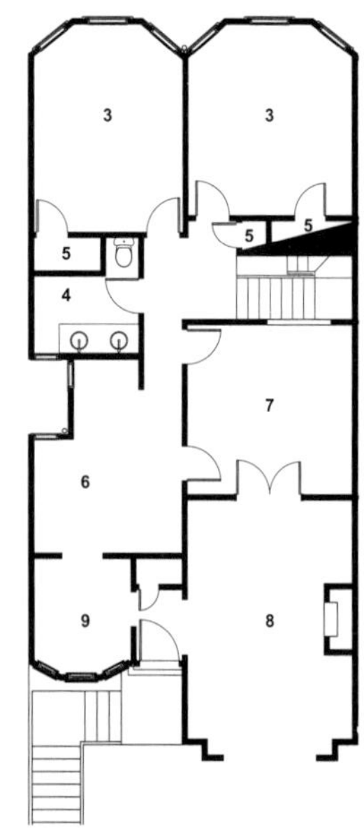

Second floor plan

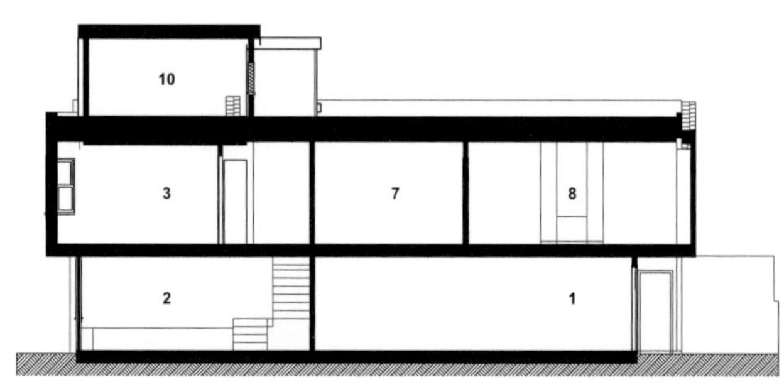

Section

MICHELE MORGAN
JEAN GABIN
DANIEL GELIN
JEAN DELANNOY

Pants
Sweats

Navigating Change in Architectural Practice

Several years ago, Dava Sobel wrote an excellent book called, *Longitude*, that described the centuries long quest for a device to accurately measure longitude while at sea. Incredibly, prior to having such a device, called a marine chronometer and invented by John Harrison around 1761 (there were multiple iterations), sailors simply did not know where they were or where they were going. It is stunning to think now that all the great explorers and mariners before the late eighteenth century were fundamentally lost and moreover, they knew they were lost. It is even more stunning to think that their awareness of their own ignorance did not stop them from setting sail on ever more ambitious adventures, so great were the potential rewards for the shrewd and the lucky.

This story contains parallels with the way that architectural practice has navigated new technologies during the past few decades and finds itself tossed about in seas of changing expectations searching for relevance and direction. Starting somewhere in the 1980's with 2D CADD software on mini and microcomputers, through the internet, worldwide web, 3D modeling and simulation, BIM, and, more recently, artificial intelligence, fast changing technology has often disoriented architectural practice and potentially threatened it both economically, and even existentially. There is a queasy feeling of being somewhat lost and tossed in all of this change, but the promise of great architecture is too strong.

In fact, however imperfectly, architects as a whole have found opportunities in many of these new technologies to become more cost efficient, improve the quality of their documents, reduce errors, and especially broaden their scope of service. For those firms that could afford the high cost and learning curve at the time, even early 2D CADD software delivered greater efficiency and improved accuracy. Later software that could cross reference multiple drawings and data bases meant architects could play a role in facilities management. The development of 3D modeling tools improved efficiency and accuracy, once again broadening the architect's potential role to provide services such as collision detection, time based simulation and computer rendering. Currently, Building Information Management, or BIM, encapsulates this idea of the architect as "keeper of the virtual building." Far from posing an existential threat to the profession, the number of US architects per capita in the US has steadily increased year over year for decades according to NCARB.

Artificial Intelligence is the latest great wave of new technology sweeping over the profession (and all of society). As a tool to improve efficiency and quality, it promises, for example, real-time code compliance checking. Seen as an existential threat, however, it promises (threatens?) to generate design permutations based on key words and code knowledge at a hallucinating speed that is unsettling. But, as unsettling as this computing power may be, who edits and prioritizes the key words? Who selects among the plan permutations? Whose imagination will be triggered by the AI output data to discover entirely new design directions never considered? Who will communicate with the client, community, consultants and other constituents? Who will move the design from something derivative to something unique?

The absorption of Artificial Intelligence into design practice will certainly impact staffing, job descriptions and responsibilities within firms, but it does not have to be a threat to practice any more than the many new tools that preceded it. Architects will find their place in this new world of AI as they have with every past technology wave because their inherent holistic three-dimensional thinking and problem-solving skills remain unique and ever more valuable.

Comparing 21st century architects with 18th century mariners may seem like a stretch, but there is nothing new about navigating with uncertainty during major technological shifts. While technology can be grand, complex and overwhelming, it is always just a means to another end, a vessel to carry us from one century to another. For architects, the ultimate goal of the profession is not to practice in one manner or another, but to make better buildings. This means practicing more efficiently and more effectively so that we, as architects, can play an even greater role in the planning and building all that is around us.

COLOMA

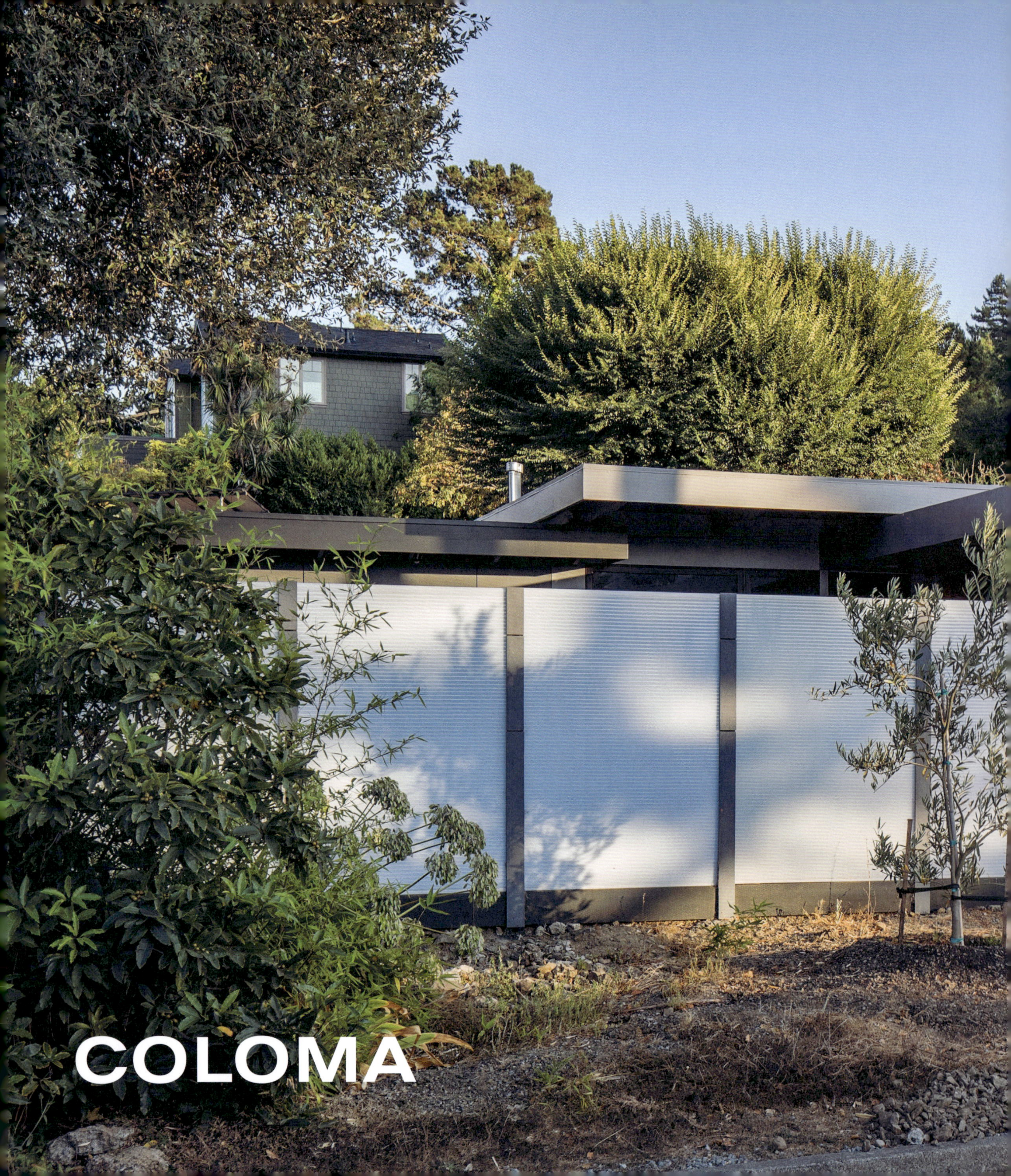

607
607

The original approximately 1800sf one-story house on this lot in Sausalito, CA was a non-descript flat-roofed tract home with carport and a vaguely "mid-century modern" vibe. Starting from this visual reference, the house is enlarged and re-imagined as a modern home with a palette of rectangular fiber cement panels and twin wall polycarbonate which accentuate its strong horizontal lines and embolden its architecture.

The carport was infilled to enlarge the living space, and a new single car garage was constructed in the front yard. The polycarbonate garage walls create a glowing lantern that welcomes visitors through the gate of the forecourt and to the front door.

The interior is an open plan that extends through the kitchen to the enclosed rear yard entertainment area. A climate-controlled wine room is the focus of the bright clean interior. Three generous bedrooms align on the northeastern edge.

Simple design gestures and a spare materials palette focus on entry and procession through space from street to rear yard. The house is transformed from a closed box to a interior moment in the fluid movement between outdoors and indoors that is possible in California's mild climate.

In every house, even the most banal and anonymous, there can be found an essence, a core concept, that can be discovered, revealed, and exploited when awoken by a new client with fresh perspective and fresh priorities. Through the renovation process, the house is reborn and finds new purpose. It gains sentience from its new owners, and they are sheltered and nurtured by its quiet presence.

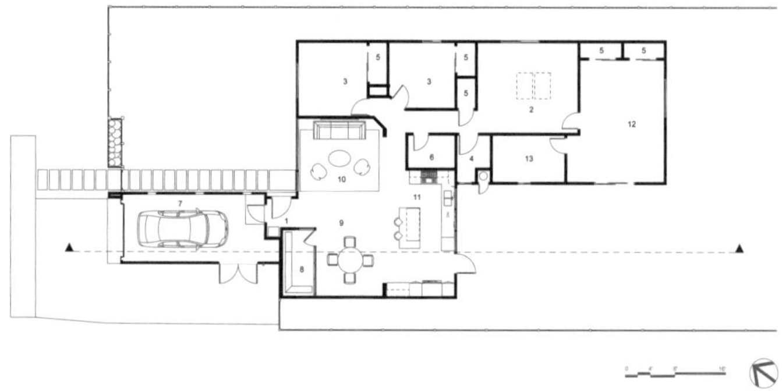

First floor plan

1. Entry
2. Family room
3. Bedroom
4. Laundry
5. Closet
6. Bath
7. Garage
8. Wine cellar
9. Dining room
10. Living room
11. Kitchen
12. Primary bedroom
13. Primary bath

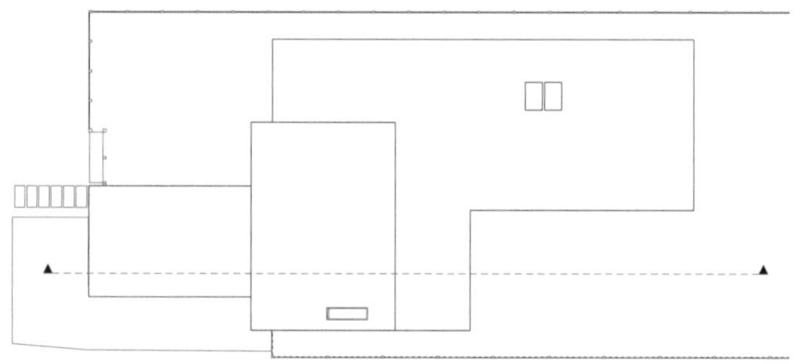

Roof plan

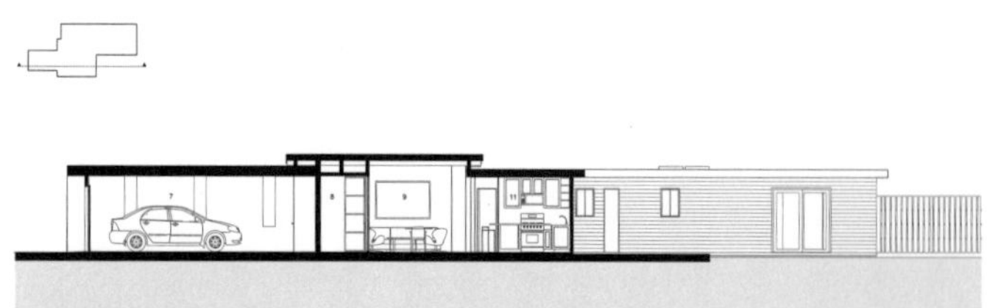

Section

607

LAC de THOUNE

Palm Springs

What is the allure of a 110 degree suburbia? Is it post war exuberance? An act of defiance against climate and logic? Is it a statement of democracy and free will? Sunstroke? Isn't it a little bit weird?

Steven Pinker authored an excellent book, *The Better Angels of Our Nature* in which he discusses people's need for a "leviathan" to bring order to society and allow it to flourish. Without such leviathans (usually referring to a government, monarch, warlord or other institution of authority) there can be chaos. Simplistically, we cede some of our rights to the leviathan in exchange for the reassurance that our neighbor has done the same and will not stab or rob us randomly. To a greater or lesser degree, leviathans place us on a more level playing field within the confines of their influence, and we derive comfort, security and identity from their embrace.

Perhaps a leviathan does not have to be an actual institution like a government or a church to exercise its authority. Perhaps it can be a powerful idea or distinct environment. Perhaps the harsh desert climate of Palm Springs acts as a great leviathan that subjugates and unites the simple tract houses of William Krisel with the rich exuberant forms of John Lautner in a single community baking under the sun. Maybe desert modernism succeeds not in defiance of its harsh climate but because of it and the order that it imposes impartially on houses and egos great and small to prioritize shelter from the sun, ventilation, low density, outdoor space, and even swimming pools.

This theory only works if combined with another great leviathan, American Democracy. Asymmetry, pragmatic plans based on living patterns, and transparency all reflect messy democratic values and appeal to one root of the American identity, self-reliance. Although many of the homes in Palm Springs are large and obviously not economically accessible to middle class incomes, because of the harsh climate, they don't employ traditional architectural forms that imply wealth or power (most of which have roots in colder northern Europe). All domestic architecture is subservient to the great desert leviathan. A butterfly roof can be perceived as an icon for old-fashioned self-made American optimism in its exuberance, both opening skyward and sheltering at same time? Or, it can just make us happy.

Pragmatism is another dimension to consider. If Le Corbusier first espoused the house as a machine for living, Palm Springs architecture, and much of US post war architecture, presents the house as an appliance for easy living. Convenience and pragmatism are also values that cut across class and are highly valued by all socio-economic groups. Palm Springs architecture presents a somewhat mythical idea that despite our origins and incomes, we all have equal access to the great outdoors, to modern kitchens and, of course, to swimming pools.

The thread of modernism from Europe to Southern California is well known. As if to give credence to this connection between Le Corbusier's "machine for living" and the far more pragmatic "appliance for living well," Palm Springs even features the "Notre Dame de BofA," a nearly perfect example of the sacred ceding to the profane. The house of worship is transformed into a city-scale ATM.

For architects, it is important to understand – as much as possible – why Palm Springs architecture or mid-century modern design generally seems to capture the imagination and uplift us. In architecture, the "why" informs the "what". If architects want to capture the spirit of a place and bring it into new forms in new places, rather than blindly cloning (as this bank's architect appears to have done!), they should step back and take time to consider whether that spirit is the result of a great climatic leviathan, or just sunstroke.

This 4500sf custom home in Palm Springs, designed for a technology executive, includes 3 bedrooms, 3 1/2 bathrooms, a large living/dining room, media room, kitchen, office and three-car garage. The front of the house is relatively closed for privacy, while the rear facade opens up to mountain views through a 27-foot-long sliding glass door. The plan unfolds around a large open living area that creates an axis through the house with bedrooms flanking it to one side, and kitchen, media room, and garage to the other.

The home's dramatic roof form takes cues from Palm Springs' "Desert Modernism" architectural tradition. At the rear, it is a dramatic butterfly form that folds and transforms into a shallow gable roof form in the front. The folded shapes and large overhangs protect the interior from harsh sun and express the spirit and optimism of this modernist community in the desert.

The single-story plan is organized around a central living space spanning front to back that offers views from the front entrance through the space to the pool and mountains. Private bedroom spaces are positioned to one side of the central spine and utility and public spaces are aligned on the other side. A see-through fireplace and heroically scaled central roof beam further reinforce this axis.

The house is planned to be "net-zero," generating as much power as it consumes. In order minimize energy consumption, the walls and roofs are highly insulated while large overhangs and vertical fins protect the south, west and east facing openings. A large 15 kwh solar array will fit discreetly on the south facing roof slope. The all-electric project will use energy efficient heat pumps for HVAC and hot water.

The house for Palm Springs is sky. The sheltering and dominant roof shapes compel visitors to look upward and consider its silhouette against the persistent blue of the sky. Gazing downwards, the sun casts powerful shadows over interesting building forms and powerful shapes appear and move across the ground. There is nothing precious about this architecture of the desert.

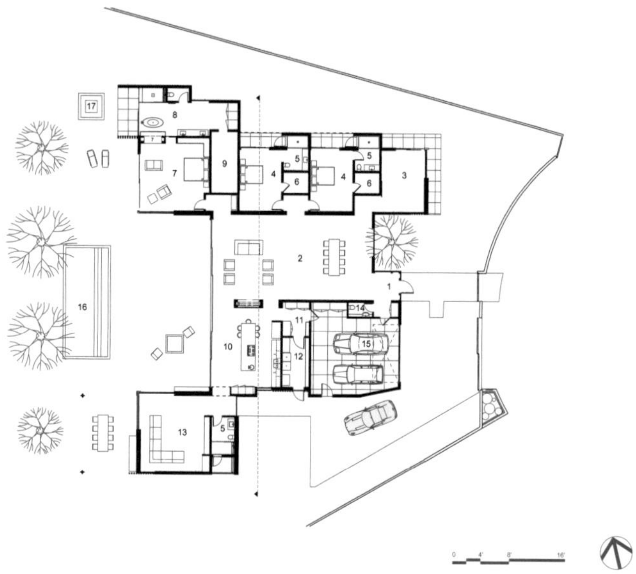

First floor plan

1. Foyer
2. Living
3. Office
4. Bedroom
5. Bath
6. Closet
7. Primary bedroom
8. Primary bath
9. Primary closet
10. Kitchen
11. Pantry
12. Laundry
13. Media
14. Powder room
15. Garage
16. Pool
17. Spa

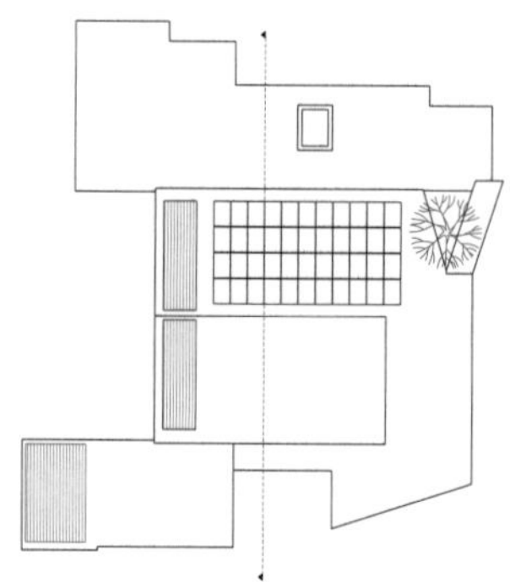

Roof plan

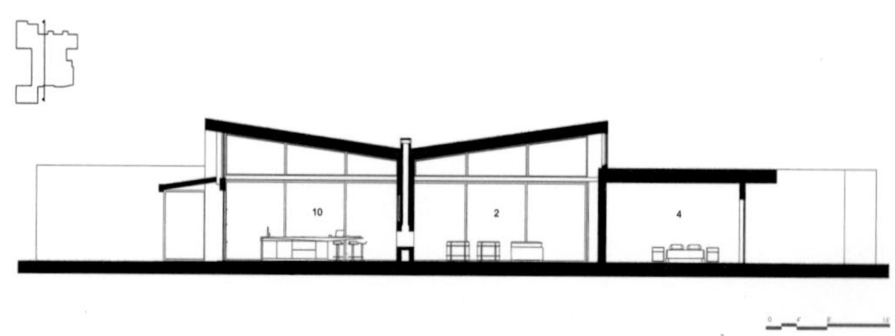

Section

3265

David Marlatt, AIA

David Marlatt, AIA graduated from the Georgia Institute of Technology in 1982 with an M.ARCH and began practicing in Atlanta with Taylor+Williams Architects where his houses and multi-family projects won national awards and publication. He obtained his architectural license at the age of 25 and soon after made the rational decision to quit his job and leave town.

He disembarked in Paris in 1986 and taught architectural design briefly before joining a local start-up software company, ABVENT, developers of 3D modeling and rendering software. Abvent quickly grew as both a developer and software distributor and, in 1987, became one of the first distributors of Hungarian based Graphisoft's ArchiCAD, the original "BIM" software. David left Paris in 1992 for San Francisco, where he served as President of Graphisoft's US office – and later as International VP of Marketing and Communications – and helped grow Graphisoft into a major worldwide player in architectural CAD software.

An Architect at heart, however, David left Graphisoft after its successful initial public offering (IPO) in 1999 to form DNM Architecture. Working throughout the San Francisco Bay Area, DNM Architecture offers a full range of architectural services from planning and programming through design, documentation and construction administration. Pushing the envelope of architectural practice and technology, the firm uses intelligent 3D CAD software to communicate with clients, translate early designs seamlessly into construction documents and manage design changes without disrupting the building process. The firm's integrated approach not only improves the final design, but produces final drawings faster and more accurately than more traditional methods.

Associations: Member American Institute of Architects, NCARB, *Chevalier dans l'Ordre des Palmes Académiques*, Former president and director Lycée Français de San Francisco.

DNM ARCHITECTURE

1A Gate 5 Road, Sausalito, CA 94965, United States | dnmarchitecture.com